THINKING THROUGH WRITING

THINKING THROUGH WRITING

GUIDELINES FOR PLANNING LEARNER-CENTERED INSTRUCTION

K. A. BEALS

ROWMAN & LITTLEFIELD
Lanham · Boulder · New York · London

Published by Rowman & Littlefield
A wholly owned subsidiary of The Rowman & Littlefield Publishing Group, Inc.
4501 Forbes Boulevard, Suite 200, Lanham, Maryland 20706
www.rowman.com

Unit A, Whitacre Mews, 26-34 Stannary Street, London SE11 4AB

Copyright © 2017 by Kathryn A. Beals

All rights reserved. No part of this book may be reproduced in any form or by any electronic or mechanical means, including information storage and retrieval systems, without written permission from the publisher, except by a reviewer who may quote passages in a review.

British Library Cataloguing in Publication Information Available

Library of Congress Cataloging-in-Publication Data
Names: Beals, K. A.
Title: Thinking through writing : guidelines for planning learner-centered
   instruction / K. A. Beals.
Description: Lanham, Maryland : Rowman & Littlefield, 2016. |
   Includes bibliographical references and index.
Identifiers: LCCN 2016028443 (print) | LCCN 2016030369 (ebook) |
   ISBN 9781475821291 (cloth : alk. paper) | ISBN 9781475821307 (pbk. : alk. paper) |
   ISBN 9781475821314 (Electronic)
Subjects: LCSH: English language-Composition and exercises. |
   Thought and thinking.
Classification: LCC PE1408 .B467 2016 (print) | LCC PE1408 (ebook) |
   DDC 808/.042071—dc23 LC record available at https://lccn.loc.gov/2016028443

Printed in the United States of America

For THOR
Seacountry Thorlyte
April 10, 1984—September 10, 1994

For COLBY
Seacountry Orion
April 12, 1994—March 22, 2009

CONTENTS

FOREWORD		ix
PREFACE		xi
ACKNOWLEDGMENTS		xiii
INTRODUCTION		xv
1	**THINKING THROUGH WRITING**	1
2	**A WRITING COURSE EXAMPLE**	9
3	**THINKING IN PREPARATORY WRITING**	53
4	**USING EXPLORATORY WRITING**	65
5	**FORMAL WRITING PERSPECTIVES**	85
6	**ULTIMATE THINKING** Independent Writing	105
7	**PROACTIVE ASSESSMENT**	117

CONTENTS

8	WRITING IN OTHER DISCIPLINES		133
9	WRITING ON OTHER EDUCATIONAL LEVELS		151

AFTERWORD	165
NOTES	167
BIBLIOGRAPHY	173
INDEX	177
ABOUT THE AUTHOR	185

FOREWORD

Writing is the vessel of thought. The power of writing is its ability to carry thoughts and ideas through vast reaches of time and distance. The written word increases our knowledge far beyond the boundaries of our own experience, enabling us to learn from the failures and successes of others ever since humans pressed the first symbols into wet clay, or penned them on parchment. Good writing, like an able ship, can carry its cargo of knowledge far and long.

Whether by a ship's log, a captain's daily record, or a traveler's diary, civilization has been advanced and enriched through good writing. The Odyssey of Ulysses as set down by the Greek poet Homer in the 8th century B.C. became the template for thousands of journeys. Records of the maritime explorations of Zheng He, Columbus, DaGama and Magellan in the 15th and 16th centuries opened up the world to itself and were the prelude to globalization. Charles Darwin's chronicle of the voyage of *The Beagle* in the 1830s began a scientific revolution still advancing today. And Joshua Slocum's memoir of single handed

FOREWORD

circumnavigation of the globe has inspired countless others to challenge themselves and the sea.

Writing is not only the vessel of thought, knowledge and information, but also the vessel of feelings. A well written novel can expand our understanding of the emotions and experiences of others. A well written scripture or poem can enrich our life, giving it greater dimension, meaning and purpose. Even a mundane memo written with some flair can make a day shimmer a little.

This volume teaches good writing as the vessel of good thinking. Like a chart or architectural drawing, good writing allows us to see the whole journey, and helps us find our way. Good writing organizes our thinking. This book charts thinking and writing, navigating to ensure that our lives will be more pleasant and productive, more instructive and more memorable.

—By Rob McCall

PREFACE

This book provides an example of a writing course, illustrating how thinking and writing converge. My purpose is to prove that thinking skills are taught best through writing. All parts of the brain and all types of learning styles are used in writing activities, simultaneously instructing thinking skills.

While instructing an undergraduate writing course, higher-order thinking about subject matter with a wide application, and problem-solving examples from Maritime Literature are used. The goal of instruction techniques is to increase thinking skills, and transfer thinking through writing across the curriculum.

The premise of the book is based on aesthetics, promoting curiosity, and influencing thinking in the learner. Four proactive elements of thinking skills instruction—Preparatory Writing, Exploratory Writing, Formal Writing, and Independent Writing—guide the process. Essays, both in short papers and in exams, as well as research papers, are the most utilized forms of writing across the curriculum. These forms of writing encourage learner insight, demonstrating thinking about content in

PREFACE

every discipline. Forms of writing specific to a discipline are enhanced in the process.

Thinking through Writing is addressed to college instructors, although useful for instructors at any educational level. The precepts of the book will increase student thinking skills regardless of discipline. The elements, examples, and guidelines for planning learner-centered instruction and positive assessment practice helps increase student engagement through writing activities, applicable in all content areas.

Instruction is easily individualized for both teachers and students. Based on aesthetics to inspire perception, the practice of thinking skills directs content and supports inquiry and reflection. Writing expresses the awareness and thought process necessary for all learning.

ACKNOWLEDGMENTS

Appreciation is due first to my students, whose positive attitude and enthusiasm in completing assignments, offering insights, and adapting concepts to their majors were unwavering, and inspired my own thinking. The forthright atmosphere throughout the college, the faculty and administration, and the superior maritime assets allow academics to thrive.

I wish to thank my colleagues for their academic contributions. My gratitude for manuscript review and thoughtful suggestions to Sally Leighton and Rob McCall. Thanks to Tom Koerner, my editor, for his assistance.

My thanks to Mark and Merlin.

INTRODUCTION

The first chapter of the book examines the connection between writing and thinking skills. The second chapter illustrates the details of the writing course. Course examples of thinking skills instruction emphasize student originality.

The writing course uses the thinking skills element—Preparatory Writing, based on student experience—discussed in chapter 3. The forms of Exploratory Writing described in chapter 4 create perceptions. In chapter 5, Formal Writing combines learner perspective with rhetorical factors for finished writing. The genres practiced accurately organize content information, thereby simplifying learning. In chapter 6, student insights on content supply self-generated questions as the focus of research in Independent Writing.

Chapter 7 describes assessment techniques, advocating the primary traits method and the Independent Writing assignment, or alternately, concisely designed subjective exams with proactive grading. Chapter 8 integrates thinking skills through writing in other disciplines. Finally, chapter 9 describes precollege and professional thinking skills through writing.

INTRODUCTION

This book provides educators with ideas of thinking skills instruction to apply, with examples of its use in an actual course. Writing across the curriculum to intensify learning, incorporate thinking, and expand and integrate content is shown to be effective in college instruction. However, the fundamental skills are applicable across the curriculum at all levels of education.

1

THINKING THROUGH WRITING

It is doubtful whether man ever brings his faculties to bear with their full force on a subject until he writes upon it.

—Cicero

Thinking is fundamental for every level of education. Writing is to thinking as learning is to intelligence.

Instructing and learning are linguistic phenomena. Language provides the basis for thinking. Words, spoken and written, develop cognition.

The meaning and use of words are exclusive content in a writing course. A writing course develops thinking skills most effectively, since thinking is the basis for writing. Janet Emig wrote:

> If the most efficacious learning occurs when learning is reinforced, then writing, through its inherent reinforcing cycle involving hand, eye, and brain marks a uniquely multi representational mode of learning. Writing involves the fullest possible functioning of the brain, which entails the active participation

CHAPTER 1

in the process of both the left and right hemispheres. Written speech thus represents a ... powerful instrument of thought.[1]

Rhetorical considerations guiding discrimination in word usage develop thinking skills: creative and critical thinking, metacognition, decision making, and problem solving. Expression in writing is the base for thought exploration, as ideas coalesce into a perspective.

Writing down a concept with important details launches the idea in the mind, offering an introduction for further consideration. More writing explores the idea, suggesting a variety of directions. As direction is expanded, reasoning with supporting points emerges as a navigational aid, guiding the initiation of a thesis or hypothesis. Writing extends cognition in all content areas. Emig adds:

> The act of writing allows the writer to manipulate thought in unique ways because writing makes our thoughts visible and concrete and allows us to interact with and modify them.... Writing progresses as an act of discovery.... No other thinking helps us develop a line of inquiry or mode of thought as completely. We can hold only so many thoughts at one time.... We lose much of what we say because it isn't written down.[2]

Using writing to instruct and improve thinking skills is most effective. The discipline of writing requires thinking to organize words in many forms. The language used to encourage thinking skills and instruct writing is singular. Its clarity and precision provide the expression of thinking and help to apply the skills while writing.

Solving writing problems emphasize organizing and incorporating prior information, rather than learning large amounts of new information. Content in other disciplines is regularly assimilated through other modes of communication as well as linguistics. Writing necessarily focuses on words.

THINKING ABOUT CONTENT

Thinking about content is implicit in all disciplines. A primary component of writing is vocabulary—the comprehension and usage of the discipline's terminology. Additionally, the history, theories, and authors are revealed when learning background, conveyed in every class and assignment. Thinking through writing, expressed in vocabulary usage and references, can be modeled on clear examples from writers within the same discipline.

Complete content knowledge may not indicate important learning in a discipline, given time limitations. "The mere learning of information is not enough; there must be the ability to think through the avalanche of facts . . . to reach an understanding of what the required information means across many dimensions," advised the University Of Vermont president Tom Sullivan in 2014.[3]

Writing Across the Curriculum, an educational movement related to writing in the disciplines and other corresponding programs that began in the 1970s, is currently reaching full development in higher education. Research on the nature of the brain and intelligence, applied to learning and instruction is extensive.

THE VISUAL BRAIN

The closest correlation to thinking is writing. Words build images corresponding to the brain's action to process information from the senses. Biologist James E. Zull explains, "Vision is central to any concrete experience that we have. In many ways, our brain is a 'seeing brain.' The brain's ability to visualize is arguably the most significant aspect of cognition."[4]

CHAPTER 1

Research shows that several parts of the brain provide different operations for processing sensory information. The sensory cortex receives signals from the senses, primarily vision. Information is sent along neurons to the back temporal cortex for viewing and then moves into the front integrative cortex where thinking originates. Thinking images are shown to the motor brain, which acts through specialized areas to produce writing, reading, and speaking.

Zull continues, "Our concrete experience of seeing is retained in a concrete form of physically connected neurons in the brain."[5] He also defines thinking: "As he organizes things in new arrangements and attaches them to the networks that represent his prior knowledge, each learner creates his own understandings. The conscious rearranging and manipulation of items in the working memory comes closest to what we call *thinking*."[6]

Experience, observation, cognition, and expression are the results of the brain's actions. Remembering from experience, seeing and comprehending, thinking and creating, and finally actions including writing and speaking are learning skills. Emotions and motivation affect the brain's processing.[7] The following page lists brain functions corresponding to thinking instruction elements.

THINKING SKILLS ELEMENTS COORDINATION WITH BRAIN FUNCTIONS

1. PREPARATORY WRITING

   Brain Activity:
   Sensory Input = Experience

2. EXPLORATORY WRITING

   Brain Activity:
   Back Temporal Cortex = Observation (Viewing)

3. FORMAL WRITING

   Brain Activity:
   Front Integrative Cortex = Cognition (Thinking + Creating)

4. INDEPENDENT WRITING

   Brain Activity:
   Motor Brain + Specialized Areas = Expression (Actions of writing, speaking, reading)

CHAPTER 1

Any course may be adapted to incorporate writing to instruct thinking skills. Instructional writing through exercising thinking skills need not restrict discipline content, or become extra work to the professor or students. Prior writing experience, including a college writing course is sufficient for practice; teaching writing in each discipline is redundant and time consuming. For example, assigning a summary to show critical thinking about a chapter's content as a substitute for a quiz does not require teaching students how to write a summary.

Writing activities in a content area apply thinking skills and assist comprehension. However, knowledge and practice of thinking skills are necessary for incorporation into a discipline, as are the writing forms representing thinking activity. Toby Fulwiler states:

> Writing resumes its natural place at the center of intellectual inquiry and exposition and becomes the clarifying companion to all the other learning activities—reading, speaking, computing, viewing and listening. Writing is basic to thinking... crucial in discovering, creating and formulating ideas, in the process we call "composing," the mental activity that characterizes our species.[8]

In addition, Ann Bertoff describes "composing as the essence of thinking."[9]

Upgrading writing is compulsory; each course requires exams and research papers, and the terminal degree process ends in a dissertation. Since writing is used in every discipline to assess, it is the best learning tool for instructing and practicing thinking skills.

Increasing thinking skills in learning activities using ideas or inquiries generated by the professor from student contributions, or directly from the student, is the foundation of learner-centered instruction. Research regarding how and when thinking skills should be taught debate separating and incorporating instruction.

Disagreement concerns instructing thinking skills without its incorporation into an academic discipline, by learning the skills separately. Some educators believe the skills may become a complex discipline, difficult to adapt for instruction and learning.

Another approach advocates instruction through incorporation, teaching thinking skills within a discipline. Students see how the skills are applied and the results, although less time is available for content instruction. Moreover, many instructors are not knowledgeable.

INSTRUCT THINKING IN WRITING COURSES

The most proficient solution is instructing thinking skills in a writing course, since language usage requires thinking. Then, incorporate the skills into other disciplines through writing activities. Insert academic specifics: from specialized documentation to traditional forms, such as a timeline in history. Academic conventions have developed through thinking skills, supporting and coordinating rather than interfering with content.

Thinking skills are essential for learning, separately or incorporated. Thinking skills integral to writing are part of the writing discipline, and as broadly applied. Thinking from all parts of the brain is expressed in a variety of genres. The genres are effective for writing in any discipline.

Writing is therefore integral to thinking skills instruction. Emig concludes,

> Writing represents a unique mode of learning—not merely valuable, not merely special, but unique. Writing serves

CHAPTER 1

learning uniquely because writing as process and product possesses a cluster of attributes that correspond uniquely to certain powerful learning strategies.[10]

Writing develops thinking skills with other disciplines. An example is using the genre of classification to sort marine species or distinguish types of ships. Instruct thinking skills through writing activities; apply the skills and activities in every discipline.

This book shows how thinking skills are used to instruct a college course. Thinking skills are invaluable for linking student experience and new information, incorporating content knowledge, as well as creating new ideas and solutions.

Thinking skills integrate all areas on all levels of learning. The next chapter examines a writing course developing thinking skills. The course uses Maritime Literature excerpts as examples for writing genres and problem solving, incorporating higher-order thinking.

A WRITING COURSE EXAMPLE

> *Aesthetics is an essential element of thinking skills programs ... develop ... a compassionate attitude towards the environment and a curiosity with which to go wondering through life—a prerequisite for higher level thought.*
> —Arthur Costa, 1987

The undergraduate Composition course at a maritime college is presented as writing and speaking in various genres. The genres increase students' writing ability not only in the class, but for future use in their majors across the curriculum. This basic required course also fulfills the seaman's requirements for the Standards of Training, Certification and Watchkeeping (STCW).

It is not coincidental that writing skills are regarded as mandatory for success in the demanding conditions of the maritime field: communication is even more vital than in earlier days. The resources and abilities required for a captain and crew with increasingly complex duties on larger or specialized ships with more valuable cargoes and higher numbers of passengers

CHAPTER 2

are compounded. Equally important is the knowledge and awareness of the marine environment surrounding mariners and influencing all actions taken. Clear, critical, and creative thinking is not optional.

A maritime college's philosophy is integrated with the ocean, and the curriculum is "primarily focused on marine related programs,"[1] as stated by the editor, Dr. John Barlow in the college catalog. The maritime curriculum offers an instant perspective. The campus is on the Atlantic, offering unlimited opportunities for experiences.

Accordingly, the background and subject for writing in this course is the sea, preferably from direct experience. A creative component is introduced from the aesthetics of the ocean environment. In the Composition course, all aspects of the sea present appropriate topics. An acceptable example of a widespread maritime writing topic is the weather, a lifelong phenomenon created by the oceans that cover over 71 percent of the planet.

COURSE INTRODUCTION

As an introduction to the course, the syllabus is reviewed in the first class. It contains the dates and activities of class meetings; the due dates of the first and final drafts of papers interspersed with revision workshops as needed; a scheduled visit to the resource center featuring the director's research seminar; and the instructor's contact information. The syllabus is the compass, a guide to the course, and is brought to every class for reference and any updating.

Individual conferences are scheduled after the research paper topic is submitted at midterm, although students may meet at the instructor's request, or whenever needed. Since little use is made in this class of the revision workshops, these are discontinued after the first; students needing assistance meet with the instructor. Also detailed is course assessment, including the Independent Writing project, worth twenty points. Due at the last class meeting, instead of a final exam, the assignment is logical and well received. Additionally stated is the expectation:

> Effective communication (written or oral) is expected to be clear, purposeful, well organized, accurate, concise, complete, and, of course, interesting to read.
> —Professor of Communications Susan K. Loomis, 2008

READING AND RESOURCES

The course syllabus lists the required writing text, the current edition of *The Prentice Hall Reference Guide* by Muriel Harris; and references an excellent Maritime Literature anthology: *The Oxford Book of the Sea*, edited by Jonathan Raban; as well as other recommended reading.

The latter specifies a best-selling nonfiction book about the modern Merchant Marine written at the instigation of Captain Andy Chase, Professor of Marine Transportation at the college, also the subject: *Looking for a Ship* by John McPhee. Listed next are Carl Safina's *Song for the Blue Ocean*, assessing the marine environment, and *In Peril*, a book by a college alumnus, Skip Strong, captain of super oil tankers and now a ship's pilot.

Others are *The Grey Seas Under* by Canadian author Farley Mowat, Joseph Conrad's *Youth*, Rachel Carson's classic *The Sea around Us*, and *The Outermost House* by Henry Beston. These books not only correspond to the curriculum on subjects from seamanship and engineering to the sciences, but they also focus on successful solutions of situational marine problems, as elaborated below:

CHAPTER 2

- *Looking for a Ship*—the clarification of a misconception about the modern Merchant Marine
- *In Peril*—the rescue of a tug and tow carrying the space shuttle by a 688-foot fully loaded supertanker
- *Song for the Blue Ocean*—the examination of modern marine environmental solutions
- *The Grey Seas Under*—the successful ocean salvages in the North Atlantic by a tug under incredibly severe conditions
- *Youth*—overcoming the disaster of a fire at sea
- *The Sea Around Us*—the warning of planet-wide devastation according to marine research
- *The Outermost House*—living on the edge of a potentially hostile environment at Cape Cod

Further reading in all other books written by the above authors is encouraged.

Apart from recommended reading, books for the class available to students on reserve at the Resource Center include all those from which quotes and other pertinent references have been used in class. Virginia Thorndike's *Bowdoin*, the history of Admiral Macmillan's century-old Arctic sailing vessel now belonging to the college, and Thorndike's survey, *Tugboats*; maritime historian Samuel Eliot Morison's *Spring Tides* describing the Maine coast, and *The Story of Mount Desert Island*, describing its history; as well as *The Mirror of the Sea* containing the incomparable essays of English maritime author Joseph Conrad, are supplementary literature.

Among general references are *The Oxford Companion to Ships and the Sea* edited by Peter Kemp, and *The Dictionary of Nautical Literacy* by R.A. McKenna. Resources are chosen to supply further information, details from the authors' perceptions, and thoughtful perspectives on maritime topics.

Writing activities continuously emphasize creative and critical thinking, decision making, and problem solving. Thinking skills activities ensure student involvement from experiences, enabling the brain to link old and new information.

THINKING IN PREPARATORY WRITING

On the first day of class, the first thinking skills element of Preparatory Writing introducing the course comprises reviewing the syllabus, the course expectations, and responding to students' questions. An evaluation begins with a metacognitive exercise.

Students produce a self-evaluation of their writing. The form is adapted from John J. Collins's effective writing plans.[2] The preprinted essay form contains sections for students to describe their writing by filling in blank spaces about:

- What they need to improve
- How they plan to improve
- What they do well

Three skills of self-assessment are thereby integrated:

- Self-planning
- Self-monitoring
- Self-evaluating

Research finds:

> When learners engage in metacognition, they develop the ability to distinguish between what they know, and what they do not... this important skill is labeled *knowledge monitoring*.

CHAPTER 2

Researchers have found a positive correlation between learner's knowledge—monitoring ability and their scholastic aptitude. Learners who exhibit the ability to monitor their learning also exhibit higher levels of scholastic achievement.[3]

Administered again at midterm, in the midst of ongoing instruction, this same form is beneficial for a thinking update. The final assessment (this form revisited) will be at the end of the course.

Next, a brief lecture on the subject of course writing: the sea. Discussion is scheduled after the students write a reflection regarding their feelings about the sea. Furthermore, the reflection is part of the instructor's objective that each session contain sustained in-class writing in addition to any quizzes, tests, exams, discussions, debates, or oral reports.

Papers are exchanged with an adjacent classmate, and reviewed. Then, class-wide discussion begins. Several volunteer students read their reflections. Finding three active captains of fishing vessels in one class is remarkable; one had participated in marine research, despite being a marine engineering major. Not surprisingly, that student becomes the highest achiever in this section of Composition.

A few students have never seen the ocean before; many are surprised at its size and the range of conditions and marine life. Marine sports, especially sailing and fishing, with some surfing, sailboarding, duck hunting, bird and whale watching are common. Several discuss the dangers of the sea, extreme weather, and notably, pirates.

ENCOURAGING INQUIRY

Class protocol is established requesting all students to question, as many as needed to completely understand anything in the course. Inquiry about the professor's paragraph

A WRITING COURSE EXAMPLE

written as the students worked revealed the topic as the sea's beauty. No one had thought about this, although the enjoyment of a sunset was mentioned in conjunction with weather on the sea.

The expectation and the importance of questions, by students for further elucidation, and by instructors to stimulate further thinking, are integral. All aspects of a topic may be examined for potential inquiry. Engaging curiosity, or an academic desire to know, will increase reasoning, improve listening, and develop better responses. Carol W. Benton further suggests,

> Metacognition is closely associated with higher order thinking skills; therefore, it is helpful to examine questioning techniques that have been shown to elicit higher order thinking from students. Teachers can use carefully phrased questions to encourage students to reveal their thought processes. In their questions, teachers give cues to students regarding the depth of mental processes needed ... there is a direct relationship between the types of questions teachers ask and the depth of thinking required by students.[4]

For example, asking a question during class requiring only recall and application limits reasoning. If the instructor inquires "What causes the tides?" A reasonable response is "the moon." Giving direction by including evident information, such as the tides are affected by gravity, asks students to think beyond basic information, inviting deeper consideration. For example, this can be achieved by asking learners "Since the moon exerts a gravitational pull on the ocean, why do the times of tides fluctuate?"

In the second answer, "the information in the response will be richer, and more in depth; therefore, the teacher will have an enriched teaching opportunity to ensure that all of the students in the class understand an important process," states

CHAPTER 2

Benton.[5] These techniques are essential in thinking skills instruction.

From their reflections, their thoughts provide ideas for future assignments, and the importance of what each student knows, has experienced, and brings to an assignment or problem is noted.

Next, ideas for writing topics related to the sea are explored and listed on the front board as students brainstorm. The contributions are also possibilities for the research paper. Additionally, the syllabus offers writing ideas. Finally, reading from the writing text is assigned for the first genre, description.

INSTRUCTING THE WRITING GENRES

Genre: Description

For out-of-class work (as needed on a preparatory basis), reading from the writing text on description prepares for instruction at the next session. The text discusses the genre of writing, its characteristics, appropriate use and strategies, preparation, and research for the writing problem to be studied.

In the second Composition class, the problem of writing a description is presented, introducing instruction; beginning with a request for questions the students may have on the textbook reading assignment. A quiz on the material covered is given, requiring the definitions and original examples of twenty-one writing terms.

Discussion of reading and writing processes, beginning with reviewing reading methods, examining the rhetorical triangle, and continuing with organizational writing patterns follow, introducing the lecture and discussion on strategies for subjective and objective description.

A WRITING COURSE EXAMPLE

Description is sensory information. Objectively, it is how the object is perceived in itself—it is factual. Subjectively, the writer gives his or her feelings about a subject—an evaluation. Specific strategies are used to create a description for both.

Reinforcing Experience

After the lecture and discussion, the second thinking skills element, Exploratory Writing recalls experience through the Learner Connection—a logbook, the simple form of maritime description. Adding complexity, a quote by American essayist John McPhee on logbooks and the use aboard ship from his book *Looking for a Ship* is distributed and read.

The Complexity Quote explores the type of description (objective) used in keeping a log (the data of a ship's activity, including speed measured in knots, through actual use of a floating piece of wood and knotted rope from which the terminology originated) and initiates further reasoning.

Students write a reflection describing prior experience with keeping a logbook. Used most often is keeping a log of a vehicle's mileage, in addition to travels, scouting experience, or a reading or learning log for other courses. The importance of a log in maritime matters is universal, and an appropriate sea-related writing example.

Closing the discussion and linking the next activity, students consider aesthetics and list five alternate words for the color of the sea. After a few minutes, examples are requested. The exercise emphasizes single words with different roots: cobalt, azure, indigo, cerulean, and sapphire (rather than sky blue) from student contributions.

These introductory activities are exploratory, leading into reading classic maritime authors' works modeling the genre. After a written summary or reflection of each literary selection, students write original examples of the genre.

CHAPTER 2

Maritime Literary Selections as Models

Handouts are distributed with a copy of descriptive passages from a contemporary American marine biologist, a nineteenth-century English naturalist, a contemporary American oceanographer, and a contemporary American naturalist on:

1. Color of water by Rachel Carson from *The Sea Around Us* (short, objective)
2. Phosphorescence by Charles Darwin from *The Voyage of the Beagle* (short, subjective)
3. Plunging breakers by Willard Bascom from *The Dynamics of the Ocean's Surface* (long, objective)
4. Fine surf by Henry Beston from *The Outermost House* (long, subjective)

The quotations are superb writing examples from classic sea literature. Other quotes may be less demanding. However, it is important that the students experience the best examples from which to learn; examples that are styles for modeling, as well as a complete variety of important sea information. In addition, the analogy between the first two excerpts and the last two is noted.

Clearness of the writing examples is imperative; only exemplary selections are chosen for instruction. Clarity in information and ideas does not exclude interesting or highly demanding content or subject variety. Thinking clearly when writing student examples of Formal Writing reinforces the perspective offered. The syllabus reinforces this attribute, by stating William Zinsser's quote: "Clear thinking creates clear writing; one cannot exist without the other."[6]

While not generally literary, data and research results offer the same opportunities as a basis for Formal Writing assignments. For example, data on the college's vessels supplied information for writing in the genre of compare and contrast.

The excerpts are given to every student to read, summarize, or reflect, then write in class descriptions, both objective and subjective, short (single paragraph) and long (a page.) The subject is the ocean, the topic of the student's choosing.

Research by Arthur Costa et al. finds:

> When higher level thinking, creativity and problem solving are the objectives, students must be in a classroom where they are in the decision making role.... The reward system in such a classroom should be intrinsic to the task.... It should be derived from internal motivation to learn—intellectual curiosity about phenomena; a striving for craftsmanship and accuracy; a desire to be a responsible, productive and independent member of a community of scholars; and a desire to emulate significant, respected others.[7]

The final thinking activity for this class is a descriptive essay on a favorite place. Finally, reading is assigned from the writing text on narrative strategies.

The second class continues thinking skills instruction in the process of solving the descriptive writing problem. The four elements of learning activities are: Preparatory Writing, Exploratory Writing, Formal Writing, and Independent Writing. A final exam as an ending evaluation may be given, although by its nature, it is content driven. Substituting an exam, however, is not as suitable for extensive thinking as an Independent Writing assignment.

Exploratory Writing: The Learner Connection

The third Composition class begins with the usual request for questions about the reading assignment. The lecturer discusses narrative strategies, noting that a narrative has

CHAPTER 2

a similar organization, but different characteristics from description. Narration is the chronological order of significant events. The subjective written form is a personal evaluation; the objective form is impersonal or scientific.

Attention is then directed to a list of transition words, the Learner Connection, from a single page in the writing text. The page is emphasized as a reference for organization and flow, especially useful when writing a narrative.

The Complexity Quote

Adding complexity, a subjective narrative quote on reclaiming the tug *HMS Frisky* by contemporary Canadian author Farley Mowat from *The Grey Seas Under* is read. After reading the selection, transition words are listed. A summary of how the transition words connect the different aspects of the narrative, and foreshadow the outcome, is written.

Formal Writing

Next, handouts are distributed with selections from the writings of contemporary American authors: a marine biologist, a marine historian, an ocean ecologist, and an essayist on:

1. A 112-foot wave by Carson from *The Sea Around Us* (short, objective)
2. The rocky Maine coast by Samuel Eliot Morison from *Spring Tides* (short, subjective)
3. A bluefin tuna by Carl Safina from *Song for the Blue Ocean* (long, objective)
4. Nathaniel Bowditch by McPhee from *Looking for a Ship* (long, subjective)

After the excerpts are read, students write a summary of each, followed with short and long subjective and objective narrations.

A WRITING COURSE EXAMPLE

Quotes from authors of increasing difficulty are chosen as models, practicing comprehension on various levels, as well as providing diversity. The range of maritime information on safety, transportation, the environment, and wildlife complements the students' study and related experiences, supplying background knowledge for thinking.

Independent Writing

The homework assignment is the first of several short papers: writing a description/narration of three-to-five pages. The first draft is due at the next class, where active revision, as needed, will occur. The final, corrected draft of the essay will be submitted a week later. An excellent paper is written by a lobsterman coming home in his boat in a storm.

CHAPTER 2

THINKING SKILLS ELEMENTS WITH LEARNING ACTIVITIES

As described above for description/narration, the instruction procedure in the Composition course incorporates the four thinking skills elements, followed for the remaining genres. Overlapping the elements are the motor brain activities of speaking, reading, and writing. Further details are in the following chapters.

1. PREPARATORY WRITING

    Brain Activity: Sensory Input—Experience for remembering
    - Assign reading homework from writing text in the prior session
    - Answer and discuss questions on the material assigned
    - Evaluate the material covered in a verbal review, written summary, or written quiz
    - Give a lecture on writing strategies for the new writing genre
    - Hold discussions and inquiries
    - This base initiates Exploratory Writing.

2. EXPLORATORY WRITING

Brain Activity: Observation—Recognition for acknowledging
- Establish the Learner Connection: a thinking experience related to the essay genre being studied
- Reinforce experience and supplement thinking with reading a Complexity Quote—related Maritime Literature or data example
- Conduct Exploratory Writing and/or discussion (class-wide or small group interaction) instigated by the Complexity Quote; recall related experiences to link old information with new
- This base initiates Formal Writing

CHAPTER 2

3. FORMAL WRITING/ORAL REPORTS

Brain Activity: Thinking—Creating for writing or speaking
- Read data or literary handouts with brief or extensive excerpts from Maritime Literature
- Write a summary or reflection of each excerpt to ensure comprehension
- Write short or long original examples of the genre modeled from the quotes
- Write an essay using a single genre, a three-to-five-page short paper combining two related genres, or present an individual or group oral report.
- This base initiates Independent Writing.

A WRITING COURSE EXAMPLE

4. INDEPENDENT WRITING: RESEARCH PAPER/ESSAY EXAM

Brain Activity: Action—Speaking, reading, writing
- Answer a topic inquiry generated by students (or the instructor in exams) from the course
- Reflect about choice explaining its significance or importance
- Hold an individual conference discussing the paper's prospectus
- Include an outline or freewriting (useful in an exam)
- Include a thesis statement (necessary in an exam)
- Provide supporting evidence: research, quotations, examples, and details (necessary in an exam)
- Include a concluding statement (necessary in an exam)
- Provide a bibliography
- Submit a first draft
- Conduct a revision
- Edit the text
- Submit a final draft

CHAPTER 2

CONTINUATION OF GENRE INSTRUCTION

Genre: Division

The next genre studied is a useful writing tool: division. Division separates information into parts with a common trait. Often initiating description, this genre offers direction.

The request for questions is pleasantly unproductive. The use of maps and charts, a common student experience, and the Learner Connection, introduces the genre of division after the lecture. It is noted that the college library is a US Depository for official maps and charts, and contains an extensive historical and current collection of documents. Reading American contemporary author C. C. Wylie's quote on the differentiation of maps and charts adds complexity.

Reflections are written from the students' experiences. Contributions in the subsequent class discussion on the former widespread use of maps for land features (topographical, motorways) and charts for water navigation are acknowledged and considered in relation to the invention of the Global Positioning System (GPS).

An extended class discussion of navigational aids such as sextant use and the necessity of charts versus GPS and other electronic devices begins. A summary of the discussion is written for future reference. This discussion is ongoing for the next few genres, and provides thoughts for later assignments.

A written summary and an in-class example of division are assigned after reading selections from an eighteenth-century American maritime author and a contemporary American marine biologist on:

1. Times of watches at sea by Richard Henry Dana from *Two Years Before the Mast*
2. Two kinds of thrills in scientific discovery by William Beebe from *The Arcturus Adventure*

A WRITING COURSE EXAMPLE

The final thinking assignment is a division essay on navigation before and after the invention of GPS. Also assigned is reading from the writing text on classification strategies.

Genre: Classification

The lecture on classification begins, after the request for questions.

Classification is widely implemented in writing across the curriculum. It is a concise method to designate content by categorizing information.

The genre of classification is introduced with a reading of Sir Francis Beaufort's 1830 wind velocity chart, *The Beaufort Scale*. The scale is the Learner Connection, familiar in weather forecasts, especially in reference to tropical storms and hurricanes. Recent weather events are discussed in relation to the wind scale. A passage about global winds by Walter Munk from his report "The Circulation of the Oceans" adds complexity.

Class conversation continues on the response of the college ships in various wind speeds. The 500-foot steel training ship, the eighty-eight-foot historical wooden sailboat and the seventy-six-foot steel tugboat are evaluated. A written summary of the discussion offers ideas for further consideration.

Literary excerpts by a contemporary American sailor and a contemporary American marine biologist as writing examples are:

1. Winds in ocean meteorology by Captain Joshua Slocum from *Sailing Alone around The World*
2. Types of plankton by Beebe from *The Arcturus Adventure*

Students write examples of division and classification, after summarizations. The importance of these genres for

CHAPTER 2

adding clarity and information, as well as the regular use of division and classification in more complex genres is established. Short papers on division/classification are assigned as before. A precise paper on types of sailboats is submitted.

Genre: Process Analysis

In the following class, after the reading review and strategies lecture, three chapters are reviewed from an alternate writing text, *The Oxford Book of Writing*.

Chapters on clarity and simplicity with writing samples—the Learner Connection—as a basis for the concision chapter are read and summarized. A reflection is written on the Complexity Quote by editor Thomas S. Kane: "Good writers help their readers, but do not assume their readers are helpless."[8] These topics are guides for the type of language to be used in the next genre of process analysis.

A written directional analysis of a process instructs the actual activity. Relevant background information is provided in the informational method. Both are the most efficient examples of critical thinking and clear writing.

Next, a directional pamphlet from the American Red Cross on survival floating is presented by the instructor, a former Red Cross Water Safety Instructor. The familiar swimming safety skill is the Learner Connection.

Survival floating is a process used when no other means of support, such as a lifejacket or survival suit, an overturned boat, or a piece of debris, is available. The process uses a minimum of movement to conserve energy; floating on the front, with outstretched arms, merely lifting the mouth above the water sufficiently to breathe, since the lungs' buoyancy keeps the body near the surface. Note that the superfluous movement of the arms or legs to raise the mouth higher is counterproductive; the opposite force drives the body deeper.

A WRITING COURSE EXAMPLE

Students then read an informative writing example. John McPhee's excerpt from *Looking for a Ship* explains dangers to merchant mariners, the subsequent use of lookouts, and the history of necessity aboard modern ships, even after the invention of radar, coordinating with the safety skill and adding complexity.

Reviewing the summaries written from previous discussions on navigational aids and wind response, the class dialogue concludes with the realization of the limits of men and mechanics against the great natural force of the sea. However, constant vigilance and the resulting safety measures invented and practiced allow successful work and exploration on the oceans. A reflection is written about all aspects of the discussion before continuing with the literary selections.

Writing excerpts from a current Maine ship's pilot, a contemporary sailor, and a contemporary oceanographer are as follows:

1. Training a third mate by Captain Skip Strong from *In Peril* (short, informational)
2. Changing burners in a steam turbine by Strong from *In Peril* (short, directional)
3. Nautical astronomy by Slocum from *Sailing Alone around the World* (long, informational)
4. Breaking waves by Bascom from *The Dynamics of the Ocean Surface* (long, directional)

After the obligatory summary, students write original examples of short and long processes. The assignment is a three-to-five-page process essay, drafts due as before.

A paper is very well written on assisting Penobscot Bay Pilots' area ships' pilots, Joseph Conrad's "trustworthiness personified." This paper describes a student's employment transporting and assisting pilots of local ships.

CHAPTER 2

Genre: Individual Oral Reports

Oral presentations are introduced after the process essay. The assignment is a five-minute speech to inform on an ocean-related experience of the student.

Instruction begins with research emphasizing student knowledge. The Learner Connection is the sea-related experience the student has chosen. Research from other sources is not required unless needed for detail clarification.

Two selections are read, adding complexity and providing short and long examples by contemporary American essayists on the following:

1. Sea stories by McPhee from *Looking for a Ship* (anecdote)
2. Life with boats by E. B. White, an essay on "The Sea and the Wind That Blows" (complete report)

One-sentence summaries are written on the selections.

A reflection is written next on actual experience to provide support. Later, the written portion of the speech is prepared as an outline, succinct notes, or any other form the student finds efficient.

Appropriate organization of the speech—introduction, body, and concise conclusion—using clear, short sentences, helps the speaker deliver significant information and interesting anecdotes, keeping the audience attentive. Quotes or statistics are only added as needed for updates.

In-class practice within small groups may ensure each student has a prior audience. While not possible for the individual reports, the group oral reports were able to coordinate the practice. Speaking in front of a mirror or before a roommate or friends is comparable.

Timed practice is essential to complete a message, as speaking past the five-minute limit is penalized. Visual aids are optional.

A WRITING COURSE EXAMPLE

Students volunteer to speak throughout the presentations given over the next few classes. Ample time for answering questions is scheduled; all students complete evaluations adapted from a rubric created by Professor of Communications Laurie C. Stone, with additional space for comments.[9] Captivating topics range from winter surfing and duck hunting to lobster research and coastal house transporting.

CHAPTER 2

MIDTERM ACTIVITIES

Two evaluations and several preparatory activities are conducted midway through the Composition course. Beginning with the Resource Center seminar, followed by research paper preparation and individual conferences, the midterm exam and midterm writing evaluation complete the exercises. All help students refresh and redirect their thinking.

The Research Seminar

The following class session is held at the college resource center, where the director presents a research seminar. Secondary sources for any academic activity requiring research and documentation include the books available on reserve, the extensive maritime book collection, the map and chart depository, peer-reviewed journals, periodicals, and newspapers.

Also discussed is the use of electronic information: instructor approval extends use to the online library catalog and available databases. Websites are limited circumspectly as allowable sources.

Because of the wealth of experts represented by the captains and professors of the faculty, interviews as a primary research source are highly recommended by the instructor, especially for up-to-date information. New information in an academic community is also easily developed from observations, surveys, and questionnaires. After the seminar, the remaining class time is used for individuals to become familiarized with the center and to locate potential sources for the research paper.

Research Paper Preparation and Individual Conferences

While developing an idea for the research paper is suggested at the first class meeting, the paper's topic is formally submitted at midterm with a written reflection on the student's choice. The thesis statement, outline, and bibliography due the class before Thanksgiving vacation are also assigned.

Individual conferences with the instructor are required at midterm to review the written or verbal prospectus, and to discuss any questions or perceived problems, paper-related or otherwise. Students met as needed during the instructor's office hours.

The instructor was also available regularly before and after class, or by special arrangement. Class protocol was reviewed, restating for the instructor's usual encouragement for inquiry.

Midterm Exam

The midterm exam consists of reading John McPhee's essay, "Travels of the Rock," from his book *Irons in the Fire*, and answering several essay questions including:

1. How does Plymouth Rock originate from several continents?
2. Is the final sentence of the essay accurate? Why?
3. Give examples from the essay of five types of writing: description, narration, division, classification, and process analysis.
4. Explain how these writing forms can be used in your major.
5. Write an example using each form from information in your major.

CHAPTER 2

Midterm Writing Evaluation

Reassigning the formatted essay of writing metacognition recognizes student progress and assesses development, alerting self-monitoring for ongoing improvement.

A WRITING COURSE EXAMPLE

RESUMING GENRE INSTRUCTION

Genre: Compare and Contrast

Reflecting midterm activities, research provides the background example for the next genre of compare and contrast. Inquiries of students regarding details about the college's vessels supply data.

Compare and contrast uses two writing methods to specify information about a subject. One is writing point by point: a single sentence or point containing a detail, followed by another sentence with a contrasting detail comparing the subject. The second writing method uses several related points combined in a paragraph or block, alternating with another block of points contrasting with the first.

After the requisite reading questions, review evaluation, and the strategies lecture, a listing of the types of the college's vessels elicits Learner Connection experiences. A 500-foot ship, a 210-foot barge, an eighty-eight-foot tall ship, and a seventy-six-foot tugboat along with a hundred other boats lining the campus waterfront or in storage, comprise the college's fleet. Complexity is added to the data by reading a passage on the modern connotations of the word "ship," by current English author John Fowles from his book *Shipwreck*.

Following the quote, student contributions (especially one midshipman's memorization) supply data on the physical characteristics of three principal college vessels, including dimensions, materials, propulsion, communications, safety features, and educational potential. The data are written on the front board for T/S State of Maine, S/V Bowdoin, and the TUG Pentagoet.

Examples of the two styles of compare and contrast writing by a current Maine ship's pilot, a contemporary American

CHAPTER 2

marine biologist, and a twentieth-century English maritime author are as follows:

1. Comparison of tugboats and ships by Strong from *In Peril* (point by point, short)
2. Comparison of a tugboat and sailboat by Joseph Conrad from *The Narcissus* (block, short)
3. Comparison of marine and land animals by Beebe, from *The Arcturus Adventure* (point by point, long)
4. Comparison of microscopic and enormous sea organisms by Beebe from *The Acturus Adventure* (block, long)

Students read the selections and summarize each, then write point-by-point and block-style comparisons of the TUG Pentagoet versus T/S State Of Maine, and the TUG Pentagoet versus S/V Bowdoin from the data.

The usual short paper on comparison and contrast is assigned as before. An absorbing paper examines historical and modern marine transportation. Preparatory reading in the writing text is also assigned for the next genre of cause and effect.

Genre: Cause and Effect

The genre of cause and effect is introduced after questions, a review, and a lecture. Writing in this genre may be informative, recounting the history and causes of action; or speculative, anticipating the possible results of an action. The genre is widely applicable across the curriculum.

The Learner Connection is the tide tables, the printed calculated times of high and low ("ebb") local tides. The tides are caused by the moon's, and, to a lesser extent, the sun's gravitational effect on the oceans, with neap and astronomically high (named "spring," although occurring in any season) tides augmenting the moon. An informative excerpt on the predictability of the tides by Samuel Eliot Morison from his book *Spring Tides* is read, adding complexity.

Literary selections from a contemporary American marine biologist and a contemporary English marine biologist are:

1. Force of the waves by Carson, from *The Sea around Us* (informative)
2. The public's devastation of tidal pools by Edmund Gosse from *Father and Son* (speculative)

A reflection and original examples of each essay form are written.

Next, an essay is written on the cause and effect of attending a maritime college. Additionally, a group oral report is assigned to illustrate use of the genre.

Genre: The Group Oral Report

Group leaders are created by the instructor, selecting the five best writers as captains. The next five rated writers are first mates, assigned by the instructor to the respective captains. The remainder of the class write their names on slips of paper and deposit these in a midshipman's white sailor cap. The captains draw names from the cap until all the class has been chosen as crew.

The Learner Connection is maritime college activities on the North Atlantic. An aspect of the activities showing cause and effect is chosen by the captains. To increase complexity, the introduction for each group report will include the root and meaning of the word denoting the aspect to be reported.

Captains choose their participation role, while each crew member researches and reports in the group panel. First mates will research and report, as well as be responsible for the

CHAPTER 2

written information reported and submitted. Group speeches individually total approximately twenty to thirty minutes.

Topics and aspects discussed are:

1. T/S State Of Maine—Aspect: Propulsion (informative)

    The college's 500-foot training ship is docked beside campus. The annual summer voyage, requisite for first- and third-year students, calls at ports around the world, from Iceland to Gibraltar. A shorter cruise in January visits East Coast and Caribbean destinations.
2. Pirates—Aspect: Weapons (informative)

    Pirates are a significant modern menace to the Merchant Marine. The group report is given the semester before Massachusetts Maritime Academy alumnus Captain Richard Phillips was abducted off the Horn of Africa by Somali Pirates and rescued in the spring of 2009.
3. Tall Ships—Aspect: Sailing (informative)

    In active use at the college, the S/V Bowdoin is a tall ship of the smaller class, now a US Historic Landmark, commanded by Captain Andy Chase. Built in Maine by Hodgton Brothers Shipyard for Arctic exploration a century ago, she has sailed back to Labrador and Greenland, where some of the inhabitants recognized the sailboat from Admiral Macmillan's earlier journeys.
4. Extreme Weather—Aspect: North Atlantic Ocean (speculative)

    The North Atlantic's comparative shallowness, and thus susceptibility to the wind, produces some of the worst weather conditions on the oceans. *The Perfect Storm*, a book by Sebastian Junger, recounts the ocean's ferocity, in which the F/V Andrea Gail, a swordfish boat out of Gloucester was lost with all crew.
5. Navigation—Aspect: History (informative)

From the ancient use of the Norse sunstone and Chinese astrolabe to improving charts with latitude and longitude, continuing with the sextant still in use, and culminating in the modern electronic inventions of Loran C and GPS, seafarers have always navigated by the sun and stars.

6. Salmon—Aspect: Vanishing Habitat (speculative)
Salmon smolt and returning adults are unable to use their native environment due to clear cutting; the wood debris is filling and polluting the streams and coastal rivers in Maine and across America.

Two weeks in and out of class time are spent preparing. Reports are thorough and well informed. Evaluations are completed by all students. One captain (of the tall ships group) is incapacitated by illness; the first mate assumes all the captain's duties, leading his group and reporting, as well as completing his responsibilities. Though unintentional, he experiences the complete function of the position.

Genre: Persuasion

The next genre studied is persuasion. Preparatory reading is assigned and reviewed. Instruction continues with the strategies lecture.

Persuasive writing convinces through deductive or inductive reasoning. All of the essay genres may be used; however, the most recently practiced three genres of process, compare/contrast, and cause/effect are effective when used in writing to persuade. Logical thinking through deductive reasoning begins from a stated generalization and moves to a specific conclusion about a topic. Inductive reasoning considers one or various characteristics to create a general statement. The types of reasoning are often used to support an argument.

CHAPTER 2

The Learner Connection is the college's research vessel, the forty-eight-foot steel R/V Friendship. Interesting sea exploration and research are discussed. A quote on seawater by current American ocean ecologist Carl Safina from *Song for the Blue Ocean* uses deductive reasoning and adds complexity. Physical facts related to the sea are brainstormed by the class, and a reflection on examples of research observations and problems is written.

Selections read next from a contemporary Maine naturalist, a contemporary American maritime historian, a nineteenth-century American essayist, and a nineteenth-century English maritime author are as follows:

1. A two day old seal pup by Henry Goodridge from *Andre the Seal* (deductive reasoning, short)
2. American Commodore Perry by Morison from *Old Bruin* (inductive reasoning, short)
3. A great mind by Ralph Waldo Emerson from *English Traits* (deductive reasoning, long)
4. English sea by Robert Louis Stevenson from *The English Admirals* (inductive reasoning, long)

A one-sentence summary of each selection, followed by original examples of persuasion using deductive and inductive reasoning, is to be written. Writing to persuade is recognized for importance in a wide assortment of forms, from letters to editors, debating, and speechmaking, to essays and Independent Writing. Persuasive writing is used in many Formal Writing assignments, notably in the genre of argument.

The assignment is the Essay Series. Also assigned is reading in preparation for the last genre.

A WRITING COURSE EXAMPLE

The Essay Series

Students read and evaluate the three quotations for the topics in the series, and write persuasive essays on each. Using information from their major, the essays convince others to disagree or agree with the quotation's inference.

The series of persuasive essays supply a preview and practice for disciplinary reasoning and writing, since the perspective is from the individual's major. Another use of disciplinary connections is in the midterm and last exam. The essays and essay exam questions require original examples of the genres written with material from the major. Additionally, the Essay Series offer an association between the short papers and the final research paper, in perspective and length. The series' topics, with a quotation, are as follows:

CHAPTER 2

Marine Resources

For the animal shall not be measured by man. In a world older and more complete than ours, they move finished and complete, gifted with extensions of the sense we have lost or never attained, living by voices we shall never hear. They are not brethren; they are not underlings; they are other nations, caught with ourselves in the net of life and time, fellow prisoners of the splendor and travail of earth.

—Henry Beston, 1928

Using information and examples from your major, write a persuasive essay agreeing or disagreeing with the quote.

A WRITING COURSE EXAMPLE

The Marine Environment

Just as the land ethic grew into the conservation and environmental consciousness of the late twentieth century, the sea ethic will logically expand our view of wildlife and its values throughout the oceans.

Such a perspective frees the mind, and opens the doors: to a lifetime of boundless inquiry to a wealth of enriching insights and reflection, to the chance to be more fully human, to the possibility of making a meaningful contribution. The only prerequisites for taking this path are respectfulness, and an extravagant desire for exploration—both impulses that build an elevated sense of vitality and purpose. The promise: that any honest inquiry into the reality of nature also yields insights about ourselves and the dramatic context of the human spirit.

For each of us, then, the challenge and the opportunity is to cherish all life as the gift it is, to envision it whole, to seek to know it truly, and undertake—with our minds, hearts and hands—to restore its abundance. It is said that where there's life, there's hope, and so no place can inspire us with more hopefulness than the great, lifemaking sea—that singular, wondrous ocean covering the blue planet.

—Carl Safina, 1998

Using information and examples from your major, write a persuasive essay agreeing or disagreeing with the quote.

CHAPTER 2

Marine Transportation

95 percent of the world's freight travels on the sea. From No. 1 in the world, the United States Merchant Marine has dropped to No. 13. American flag companies sail under heavy overheads of taxes, insurance rates, and crew costs. We pay other flags, including Russia, millions of dollars to deliver our foreign aid: rice, flour, vegetable oil, powdered milk, tanks, jeeps. By law, fifty percent is supposed to go on American ships, but we don't have the bottoms. Some years, we carry five percent. Even so, our shipping companies are more dependent on our foreign aid than the foreigners we aid.

—Captain Paul M. Washburn from John McPhee, 1990

Using information and examples from your major, write a persuasive essay agreeing or disagreeing with the quote.

A WRITING COURSE EXAMPLE

Owing to limited time, only a page or two is completed on each of the topics. Yet, this assignment creates individual, in-depth perceptions through writing with information from other disciplines. While assigning the series earlier in the course may allow more time for consideration of the topics; thinking preparation is insufficient until most of the course is completed; as seen in the first exercise of the argument genre. Furthermore, the genre of persuasion is presented near the end of instruction.

However, since the thinking revealed is invaluable, the topics and quotes should ideally be posted at midterm for metacognition, as the topics do not specifically interfere with the research paper increment.

Genre: Argument

Following questions on the assigned preparatory reading for the genre of argument, the textbook information is evaluated through a quiz of twenty-five definitions with original examples. Instruction continues with the strategies lecture.

Argumentative writing begins with a claim: a statement of a value, policy, or fact. The Learner Connection is the sea's importance. Further acknowledgment of the sea's influence is the large body of literature and well-known authors' writings about the sea, found in the college library's extensive maritime collection. The existence of the maritime colleges and training, certification, and historical importance are additional reinforcement.

Complexity is created by Charles Darwin's quote on the "illimitable ocean." The ocean's prominence is accentuated by its beauty in storm or calm. The aesthetic quote introduces another positive characteristic of the sea. The claim is read, asserting the sea is a sanctuary, a value appreciated by a

CHAPTER 2

contemporary Maine naturalist in a second excerpt from his memoir, *Andre the Seal.*

> I have lived all my life by the sea. I can't imagine myself living anywhere else. Inland people live in the midst of change they can do nothing about. The sea you can count on; it will always be there. Petty problems may be thorning you ashore, but once you head out into the bay, you can shuck everything off. The sea is a sanctuary.
> —Henry Goodridge, 1975

The warrant of the argument, from the evidence he offers to support his belief, opens a class-wide discussion about the quote.

In contrast to the Composition course's initial class, every student offers examples of sea-related topics. Interaction using thinking skills supplies experiences related to marine information, often reflecting the components of the literary selections given as examples. Since the selections offer a nautical perspective, practice in informal and Formal Writing assignments expands student perceptions. Now, ideas about the sea produced through initial exercises and writing about the genres as well as additional learner-centered activities are extensive. Each student lists five or more aspects of marine significance.

In writing an argument, the warrant—a fact, policy, or value—links the claim to supporting evidence—an assumption, principle, or belief, respectively. If various fallacies in reasoning are avoided, the warrant and its criteria may be accepted and established.

Reasoning in the genre of argument may be misled by hasty generalizations or circular reasoning, non sequitur, or false analogy. Other errors—through doubtful causes, related "bandwagon" support, either/or reasoning, or personal detail diversions—invalidate an argument.

A WRITING COURSE EXAMPLE

Argument uses logical reasoning, deductive or inductive, usually with cause and effect or problem-solution organization. Presenting the claim, evidence, and warrant uses critical thinking to gather and present evidence. In argument, evidence is proof developed through persuasive writing.

Literary examples from a current American ocean ecologist, a contemporary Canadian maritime author, and a contemporary Maine author are:

1. The ocean's appearance by Carl Safina from *Song For The Blue Ocean* (belief)
2. War time recognition by Farley Mowat from *The Grey Seas Under* (principle)
3. Intellectual accomplishments in northern latitudes by Kenneth Roberts from his essay "Don't Say That About Maine" (assumption)

All the quotes are summarized, then analyzed for the claim, warrant, and reasoning in argument. Original examples of arguments are written over the next two classes.

An argument and persuasion paper is assigned, drafts submitted as before. Topics examined range from the seaworthiness of survival suits—since they are not shark proof—to whether ships carrying humanitarian aid should fly the flag of the country to which the aid is destined, to dissuade pirates and avoid delays.

COURSE COMPLETION

Last Exam

Assigned during the week of Thanksgiving vacation are final readings from the writing text. The readings review rhetorical considerations for writing in other disciplines.

CHAPTER 2

The test on the last three writing genres is given this week, created from a selection on seamanship from Joseph Conrad's XXXVI Essay from his book, *The Mirror of the Sea*. Students read the selection, and then write their responses to the following statements and questions, including:

1. Give the claim, support, and warrant of the selection.
2. Write a reflection of how the seaman's awareness of safety is developed through the incident.
3. Give examples by Conrad of compare and contrast, cause and effect, and argument and persuasion.
4. How can the genres be used when writing in your major?
5. Write an example of each genre using information from your major.

The Research Paper

At the class meeting before Thanksgiving vacation, the thesis statement, outline, and bibliography for the research paper are submitted. A quiz is conducted on the types of research necessary for the various types of Formal Writing and speaking assigned in the course. The writing assignment over the holiday is the first draft of the long paper.

After vacation, the first draft of the paper is submitted. Throughout the course, activities in preparation for the project are assigned and prepared as mentioned. Dividing the parts of the paper with due dates ensures that the work is scheduled into manageable amounts for complete thinking development.

The basis for the paper is a question the student has about a marine-related subject, forming the thesis. If general information is desired about the topic, perspective showing why this is of interest is developed, rather than merely summarizing knowledge or listing data.

A WRITING COURSE EXAMPLE

Exploring an interesting aspect demonstrates inquiry, further justifying significance with specific evidence and detailed examples. Experience in developing topics in the Composition course is practiced in Exploratory Writing, extended class or group discussions, as well as when composing the short papers, including the Essay Series.

Bringing thinking skills through writing to a topic create a clear perspective inspiring insight. Papers received examine topics from the Large Hadron Collider and the importance of ships' pilots to oil rig structure and commercial fishing. Through writing, students confirm their interest and add insight.

Requiring a research paper offers an opportunity for exploring the myriad interests an individual brings to academic inquiry. Complementary to a writing course, Independent Writing is the culmination of thinking skills. Furthermore, research projects prepare a learner by building experience and knowledge to transfer across the curriculum.

A second semester of writing would be ideal to address the research paper and other complex writing. However, this college has a course on Research Methods, and an Advanced Writing course for further preparation. Additionally, a Capstone Project is required in senior year to thoroughly correlate education and careers.

Last Class Meeting

Assorted evaluations are completed at the final meeting of the Composition course, after the research paper is submitted.

- The writing evaluation form is revisited to conclusively assess individual writing development and accomplishment.
- An instructor evaluation is completed, collected, and immediately returned to the dean's office.

CHAPTER 2

- A summary of the eleven genres studied is written, with five individually selected as the most useful.
- A survey/discussion evaluates the reading selections for content and interest.

Writing using thinking skills—from metacognition, creative, and critical thinking including problem solving and decision making, to analysis and final evaluation—appropriately conclude the course.

A WRITING COURSE EXAMPLE

USING MARITIME LITERATURE

And the sea shall grant each man new hope.
—Christopher Columbus, c. 1492

Maritime Literature selections in the Composition course offer ideal examples for thinking and writing. The majority of subjects concern problems and subsequent solutions in a marine environment. Moreover, critical thinking is well described in the diverse circumstances mariners encounter.

In the August 2015 issue of *Proceedings*, an independent forum of the Sea Services, the featured interview with about-to-retire Admiral James A. Winnefield is titled "You Have to Be a Good Thinker."

Questioning by the interviewer begins, "You started writing as a midshipman. As far as thinking beyond your particular world, how did you get... those larger ideas and start pursuing more than the minimum requirement?"

Winnefield answers, "I went from a junior officer tour to... an instructor at Top Gun and a department head tour.... From there, I went to the Joint Staff, where I was briefing General Colin Powell."

Asked next, "How important is writing to reach other people?"

Winnefield replies,

> Writing was important partly because to be a good writer, you have to be a good thinker. There is something about the discipline of trying to write that's hard work. It really clarifies your thinking and organizes your thought process.... You'll start to see that you interpret things in a different way than the people around you.... I was writing about what I was doing at the time. It led me to coin one of my favorite sayings: "Incredibly bright adults will work incredibly long hours perfecting

CHAPTER 2

fundamentally flawed concepts." That's exactly what we were doing at the time. To break us out of that kind of behavior was what I was trying to get done with some of the writing.... We've got to get creative about how we operate in the world, how we think[10]

A column in the same issue advocates "Constructive, Not Disruptive Thinking," by Navy Commander Harrison Scramm. Scramm states, "There is only one surefire way to get new ideas adopted: Be so good, so well thought out, and so articulate that they simply cannot be ignored."[11]

Eight essay contests are currently open at the forum, including a standing offer with thousands of dollars of prizes for essays "for those who dare to read, think, speak and write in order to advance the professional, literary and scientific understanding of sea power . . . to discuss the most compelling and forward thinking ideas. There is no restriction on theme."[12] Judged in the blind, by a board composed of serving Sea Services professionals in 1994, Admiral Winnefield (then Commander) won first prize.

Coordinating with the college's maritime curriculum, Maritime Literature is ideal background content. Additionally, incorporating Maritime Literature connects students to our accomplishments and inimitable maritime heritage.

Extensive training for thinking is part of lifelong student success. Writing instruction through Maritime Literature emphasizing thinking skills is an integral part.

THINKING IN PREPARATORY WRITING

> *Language represents the most available medium for composing; in fact, the significance of sheer availability in its selection as a mode for learning cannot be overstressed.*
>
> —Janet Emig, 1977

Appropriately, the first element of thinking skills instruction is Preparatory Writing. The element reviews, establishes, and presents information.

The components useful for instruction are as follows:

1. A reading assignment or research/recall.
2. Encouraging inquiry about the assignment, instructor response, and brief discussion.
3. Evaluating the assignment material.
   Reading/recall: written evaluation
   Less extensive or complex reading/recall: verbal review
4. Brief lecture on content.
5. A reflection or other written response.
6. In-depth discussion, including individual notes or summary.

CHAPTER 3

Each of the components prepares the student through a thinking exercise.

Thinking instruction will focus and refine reasoning. The first element assists comprehension, applies Learner Preknowledge of content, and begins inquiry, offering guidance for responses.

PREPARATION FOR COURSE INTRODUCTION

A course syllabus is useful for every educational level. Among other information, the syllabus introduces the subject, details major concepts in the course, and lists learning activities, so students are aware and informed, and may hold an instructor accountable. Stimulating students that are engaged, as well as those less competent in a discipline, the syllabus links the student's environment with the academic community and its resources.

Review and summarization of pertinent information supplied in the syllabus is not the only preparation necessary for a course. Thinking exercises in each discipline on every level provide intellectual direction.

After the syllabus review, a problem or inquiry on disciplinary content may be presented to the class as an introduction to the direction of the course. Or a question on the interests and intentions of the learner, or Learner Preknowledge may be asked. More suggestions for questions, including those specific to a discipline, on course introduction by Professor Alan Marwine are listed in chapter 8.

In the Composition course introduction, self-knowledge is recalled. The first thinking exercise of Learner Preknowledge in the Composition course evaluates individual writing ability.

THINKING IN PREPARATORY WRITING

An exercise using metacognition is assigned for self-evaluation: perceived learner's competence in a discipline. Guided by a preprinted essay format, with blank spaces to fill, the metacognitive exercise is completed and submitted.

The brief lecture that follows presents the knowledge that the subject for all course writing is the sea, including aesthetic considerations, and coordinating with the college's maritime curriculum. A written reflection on in-depth Learner Preknowledge—students' experience and thoughts about the sea—is assigned for in-class writing. The papers are exchanged between pairs of students for examination and commentary, before a class-wide discussion begins.

The information generated prepares for Exploratory Writing. Furthermore, topics are suggested for the final course evaluation—Independent Writing of a research project.

At the end of the first Composition class, preparatory reading is assigned from the Composition textbook. Important rhetorical methods and the introduction of writing strategies in the essay genre of description are reviewed for the next class. A template and example for course introduction is on the next page.

CHAPTER 3

PREPARATION FOR COURSE INTRODUCTION TEMPLATE

1. Syllabus Review for the Course Titled: _____
2. Learner Preknowledge Reference: Inquiry/Content Problem: _____
3. Evaluation: _____
   _____
   _____

4. Lecture: _____
   _____
   _____

5. Response: _____
   _____

6. Discussion: _____
7. Assignment/Preparation for Next Class: _____

   Reading: Textbook: _____
   _____
   Supplementary Texts: _____
   _____
   Other Material: _____
   _____
   Writing: _____
   _____
   Thinking: _____
   _____
   Research: _____

THINKING IN PREPARATORY WRITING

COURSE INTRODUCTION EXAMPLE

1. Syllabus Review for the Course Titled: *Composition*.
2. Learner Preknowledge Reference: Inquiry/Content Problem: *Writing experience of learners*.
3. Evaluation: *Metacognition: self-evaluation, monitoring, and planning of writing ability*.
    What I need to improve, how I plan to improve, what I do well when writing (formatted essay).
4. Lecture: *For all assignments, write about the sea and related topics. For example, the lifelong experience of weather, influenced by the sea which covers over 71 percent of the earth, is a valid topic*.
5. Response: *Written reflection on learner experience of the sea and related thoughts*.
6. Discussion: *Individual and notable sea experiences*.
7. Assignment/Preparation for Next Class: *Reading on writing methods; strategies for description writing*.
    Reading: Textbook: *p. 1-30* Supplementary Texts: *None*
      Other Material: *Review syllabus*
    Writing: *Take notes on ideas for projects and observations as needed*.
    Thinking: *Ideas for course writing and the Independent Writing project*.
    Research: *Observe the sea and weather*.

CHAPTER 3

PREPARATION FOR INSTRUCTION

The components of Preparatory Writing organize instruction: the reading/recall assignment, student inquiry and instructor response, evaluation of assignment, lecture, written response, and discussion.

Beginning with the assigned reading, research, or observation, students receive new material—strategies for writing the genre of description—or review content, such as rhetorical methods in Composition. Occasionally, recall from experience is assigned. However, recall is prevalent and most constructive in the course introduction.

Textbooks providing a compilation of established and updated disciplinary content are the usual instructional base. Students are responsible for the material contained in the text, although it may be supplementary to the instruction. Limited, or actively incorporated in instruction, the content is often evaluated during midterm and final exams, in addition to recommended reading of supplementary texts and other material.

Available on reserve at the college Resource Center are recommended books, and incidental reading for further details and viewpoints. Supplementary texts are often a springboard for ideas, research, and Independent Writing.

On the college level, a text is primarily a useful reference. Along with supplementary texts, recommended reading, and incidental materials, the instructor's knowledge guides content. The text is the basis for review of content and further research. Specific answers for lapses in knowledge, for example, in writing: how to effectively incorporate transition words, or punctuate participle phrases are offered. Familiar practice in any discipline includes refreshing vocabulary with the glossary, and reviewing the bibliography for a listing of secondary research sources.

THINKING IN PREPARATORY WRITING

Therefore, a text reading assignment assists instruction. A text offers a comprehensive foundation from which to draw many instructional points, supplying an informative review to introduce a variety of disciplinary content. Supplementary literature, or other sources illustrating specifics, support advancement in instruction.

As stated in chapter 2, inquiry in every area is continuously encouraged. Inquiry leads to perceptions, and extends thinking. In Preparatory Writing, the instructor's response to the students' questions related to the reading assignment ensures comprehension, and includes a brief discussion for clarification.

As scholars—active participants in a thinking environment—considerations entail:

- Aesthetics
- Environment at school, home, and community
- Competent literacy in the language of instruction
- Empathetic response to challenges
- Unlimited typical and atypical possibilities for problem solutions

This includes being prepared at all times for a thoughtful evaluation. An evaluation of the knowledge from the assigned textbook reading is conducted before the lecture in the second class of Composition.

A verbal review may be sufficient. However, a written evaluation is especially beneficial for thinking:

- At the beginning of a course
- To reestablish incompletely recalled knowledge
- For lengthy topics
- For a more complex topic
- For noting interesting details or background

CHAPTER 3

A written subjective evaluation requiring originally composed responses—a definition or example—activates reasoning. The first Composition course quiz required twenty-one writing terms to be defined with original examples. The evaluation is submitted, and is an additional tool for assessing Learner Preknowledge of the topic.

Next, a lecture presents content: strategies for composing in the first genre of description. Since writing and methods are also the content in Composition, learner interaction is expected. However, in every discipline, active learning through writing is an opportunity for thinking.

An interval after the lecture is allowed for response, inquiry, and discussion. The written reflection assigned details Learner Preknowledge. Clarifying, and supporting the information introduced by the instructor; a reflection; or a similar exercise verifies content and stimulates contributions to the class discussion. Furthermore, thinking for Exploratory Writing is initiated.

Therefore, every student must think, although not necessarily vocalize. If extensive, notes, or a written individual summary of the discussion—important for student comprehension and to acknowledge any self-originated ideas—may be necessary to record important directions.

Containing learning styles of visual, auditory, and kinesic modes in the thinking activities from the element of Preparatory Writing, information is provided for incorporation of the remaining elements. Increasing thinking when instructing a new concept inspires ideas.

Useful forms for preparatory writing and thinking are listed on the next page, followed by a template and example for course instruction.

PREPARATORY WRITING FORMS

- Applying
- Connecting
- Coordinating
- Defining
- Details
- Examples
- Explaining
- Fill-in forms
- Illustrating
- Identifying
- Inquiring
- Metacognitive exercises
- Notetaking
- Observing
- Recalling
- Reporting
- Responding
- Summary
- Terminology—acronyms
- Vocabulary

CHAPTER 3

PREPARATION FOR COURSE INSTRUCTION TEMPLATE

1. Instruction Topic: _____
2. Assignment Reference: _____

    Reading: Text _____ Supplementary Texts: _____
       Other Material: _____
    Writing: _____
    Thinking: _____

    Research: _____
3. Learner Inquiries—Area(s) for Clarification: _____

4. Evaluation of Assignment: _____
    Written Response: _____
    Verbal Review: _____
5. Lecture Summary: _____

6. Discussion Focus: _____

    Class: _____
    Group: _____
    Pairs: _____
    Combination: _____
7. Content coordination with the next thinking skills element of:
    Exploratory Writing: _____ Formal Writing: _____
       Independent Writing: _____

COURSE INSTRUCTION EXAMPLE

1. Instruction Topic: *Writing in the genre of description.*
2. Assignment Reference: *Reading on rhetorical methods and description writing.*
   Reading: Text: *p. 1-30* Supplementary Texts: *None* Other Material: *None*
   Writing: *Notes as needed.*
   Thinking: *Sensory information: colors, changes, sizes, shapes; interesting nautical topics.*
   Research: *Sea-related writing ideas and observations.*
3. Learner Inquiries—area(s) for clarification: *Varies with class.*
4. Evaluation of Assignment : *Quiz.*
   Written Response: *Twenty-one definitions and examples of writing terms.* Verbal Review: *No.*
5. Lecture Summary: *Strategies for writing objective and subjective description.*
6. Discussion Focus: *Types and characteristics of description writing.*
   Class: *Yes*
   Group: _____
   Pairs: _____
   Combination: _____
7. Content coordination with the next thinking skills element of:
   Exploratory Writing: *Yes* Formal Writing: _____
   Independent Writing: _____

CHAPTER 3

THINKING FOCUS

The thinking skills element of Preparatory Writing precedes the three remaining thinking instructional elements assessing Learner Preknowledge. Activating reasoning about any topic, whether introducing a course, instructing a disciplinary concept, or any discipline's learning exercise on any educational level benefits from applying the components of the first thinking skills element.

The focus on thinking through a written evaluation of an assignment with related reading or recalling established information coordinates with new information in the lecture. The lecture and subsequent class discussion form the basis for the second thinking skills element of Exploratory Writing.

The first Preparatory Writing form listed is applying, and begins with identification. Once specified and defined, a valid concept elucidates disciplinary content. Providing background, as well as pertinent evidence, application illustrates the use of the material. For example, the observation affirming the earth's resemblance to a sphere helps to define the demarcation of latitude and longitude.

Further discussed in chapter 4, exploring by thinking through writing creates perception. Refine thinking by choosing noteworthy original ideas from Exploratory Writing to support an interesting perspective when writing in an essay genre. The perspective in Formal Writing offers a direction for understanding, creating insight in Independent Writing.

Expanding an idea through thinking begins with the Preparatory Writing thinking skills element, and advances through writing.

4

USING EXPLORATORY WRITING

The human brain is a learning organ; learning is what it does. The main task for the teacher is to find the connections.

—Biologist James E. Zull, 2002

Learner-centered instruction incorporates the experience of the student. Thinking skills instruction builds on the integration of student experience. Emig observed, "Written verbal language requires the establishment of systematic connections and relationships."[1]

The second thinking skills element of Exploratory Writing uses a learner's experience to link old and new information. The Learner Connection is developed through writing.

Emphasizing expressive writing across the curriculum "can be startling . . . in terms of the changed nature of learning, in the increased validation of the personal experience of the individual writer, and in the increased creativity and elaboration of ideas that can emerge in student writing,"[2] states John C. Bean. Additionally, providing time and ascribing importance to

CHAPTER 4

examining a subject using Exploratory Writing creates factors adding perspective for finished thinking in Formal Writing.

The methods to select, prepare, and incorporate thinking and writing assignments begin with thinking exercises. Exploratory Writing introduces a writing genre by connecting with student experience, and then increases complexity with a related quotation, suggestion, or question. John Dewey wrote:

> Teachers have a responsibility to serve as guides for learning by setting up opportunities for learners to exercise curiosity and make connections that lead to reflective thought. We do have to learn *how* to think well. Especially *how* to acquire the general habit of reflecting.[3]

In the second class of Composition, thinking introducing the genre of description uses the learning activities listed in the first thinking element of Preparatory Writing: a reading assignment; brief inquiry and response; a written evaluation, lecture, and discussion. Preparatory Writing exercises aid comprehension and support Exploratory Writing.

EXPLORATORY WRITING ACTIVITIES

Instructing the essay genre of description is introduced with keeping a logbook, a simple form of description, and the Learner Connection. Reading McPhee's logbook quotation increases complexity, and writing a reflection of students' use of a logbook uses critical thinking. The logbook is a universal maritime exercise.

Biologist James E. Zull explains:

> We need reflection to develop complexity. We may start with a direct and ... relatively simple concrete experience, but that

experience grows richer as we allow our brain the freedom to search for . . . connections. As we find those connections, our brain changes. We attach the networks of our present experience to those that represent our past experience. The art of directing and supporting reflection is part of . . . leading the student toward comprehension.[4]

Exploring the topics reconnects with the learner's life experiences. Dewey advised:

> Build on experience . . . select those topics that have potential. . . . The educator, more than any other profession, must be concerned to have a long look ahead. Connectedness in growth must be his constant watchword.[5]

Writing develops further connections, reinforcing experience and allowing time to contemplate and recall aspects of a topic.

Furthermore, Exploratory Writing demonstrates a variety of thinking skills with which to interact and begin instruction. Forms from analogy to freewriting to keeping journals to title seeking, entail thinking more intensively. Thinking on paper through Exploratory Writing expands perception and offers new ideas. Integrating thinking skills with disciplinary content through Exploratory Writing assists comprehension and increases knowledge.

Some Exploratory Writing forms applicable across the curriculum are listed below. Which forms will assist students in achieving your instructional objectives?

CHAPTER 4

EXPLORATORY WRITING FORMS

- Analogies
- Brainstorming
- Creative writing
- Drama
- Exploring word origins: through context, disciplinary terminology, linguistics, synonyms
- Fiction
- Freewriting
- Interactive electronic blogs
- Journals and diaries
- Linking: diagrams, idea maps, webs
- Listing
- Metacognitive exercises
- Nonfiction
- Outlines
- Poetry
- Prospectus
- Reflections
- Review
- Summary
- Thesis statements
- Title ideas

THINKING IN ACTIVE EXPLORATORY WRITING

Creating analogies—listed first of the forms—along with metacognitive exercises, all creative writing forms, and investigating the origins of words are the most intensive thinking forms of Exploratory Writing. Each form requires the brain to form extensive new thought patterns.

The reaction to thinking about a topic in a new way, or investigating and finding a new fact providing a fresh view, influences perceptions. For example, examining the roots of words to find the origins, developed from seemingly distant languages or concepts from the past, creates interesting ideas from reactions, offering new directions for thinking.

Exploratory Writing encourages perceptions, which become ideas. The forms listed help introduce thought patterns leading to other concepts. Making a link through experience, as a Learner Connection, then increasing thinking through a Complexity Quote adds related, though different concepts. Thinking encourages more exploration through writing, refining the previous focus presented in the first element of Preparatory Writing.

While word origins discover background depth, especially intensive are analogies, requiring critical thinking about coordinating words, and placing the words in a relationship that defines the words and explains the connection. An example: A waterspout is to the sea as a tornado is to land.

Critical thinking in analysis, evaluation, and synthesis is necessary; problem-solving skills are part of writing or completing an analogy. An analogy is an interesting and effective example of stimulating ideas through Exploratory Writing.

CHAPTER 4

EXPLORATORY WRITING THINKING EXERCISES

Writing genres offer different types of expression to organize thinking about content. An example is the established use of classification across the curriculum. The Composition course begins with description; learner awareness, including consideration of aesthetics, personifies observation.

Below are the genres taught in the Composition course, with the Learner Connection, and Complexity Quote in Exploratory Writing exercises also listed. The exercises are introductory thinking for Formal Writing. On the last pages, a template for thinking and writing activities, and an example are provided for incorporating Exploratory Writing in your discipline, with suggestions from the Exploratory Writing Forms list.

1. Essay genre: Description

    LEARNER CONNECTION: Logbook
    - Complexity increases by reading a description of a log from *Looking for a Ship* by John McPhee. The selection explains the information contained in a ship's log and reviews circumstances, surroundings, historical origin, and modern use
    - Review of experience with keeping a log
    - Reflection written of own logbook use
    - Definition of words for the sea's color
    - Listing five synonyms for the color blue, emphasizing roots of words

2. Essay genre: Narration

   LEARNER CONNECTION: Transition words
   - Identification and use of transition words
   - Review of the transition words list in the current writing text, and writing significance for coherence and unity
   - Creating complexity through reading a narration on reclaiming the tug *HMS Frisky* by Farley Mowat from *The Grey Seas Under*
   - Summary written showing how transition words order the narration and influence the outcome

CHAPTER 4

3. Essay genre: Division

    LEARNER CONNECTION: Maps and charts
    - Reading about the difference between maps and charts from an excerpt by C. C. Wylie, adding complexity
    - Reflection written of own map and chart use
    - Noting the college Resource Center is a US Depository for maps and charts
    - Identification of the depository as a primary source for reference, research, and writing topics
    - Ongoing discussing of the necessity of sextants, maps, and charts versus GPS and other electronic aids.
    - Noting the contribution to navigation of Nathaniel Bowditch through his world-renowned book *The American Practical Navigator*, now known as *Bowditch's Navigation*
    - Identification of transportation professor Captain Andy Chase as an invaluable primary source for interviews, reference, research, and writing topics. Captain Chase is a descendant of Nathaniel Bowditch, owns Bowditch's original sextant, and is the subject of John McPhee's book on the modern Merchant Marine: *Looking for a Ship*. He is also the author of a collection of modern sea stories
    - Summary written of the navigational aids discussion for future reference

4. Essay genre: Classification

   LEARNER CONNECTION: *The Beaufort Scale* invented by Sir William Beaufort in 1830
   - Reading *The Beaufort Scale* with categories of wind speeds
   - Identification of the sea as the primary influence of climate, covering over 71 percent of the earth
   - Discussing recent weather—autumn hurricanes and tropical storms—in relation to the scale
   - Reading a quotation by Walter Munk on global winds and currents, adding complexity
   - Reflection written of familiarity with the scale from weather reports and events
   - Estimating the response of the college's vessels in various wind speeds: the 500-foot steel training ship, the eighty-eight-foot wooden historical sailboat, and the seventy-six-foot steel tugboat
   - Summary written of the wind speed discussion for future reference

CHAPTER 4

5. Essay genre: Process Analysis

   LEARNER CONNECTION: Survival floating
   - Review of survival floating experience
   - Reading a directional pamphlet from the American Red Cross on survival floating
   - Discussion and instruction of process and details presented by the professor, a former Red Cross water safety instructor
   - Review information on how and when to perform survival floating
   - Increasing complexity by reading about the dangers at sea to merchant mariners and the necessity of posting ships' lookouts, even with radar and electronic inventions, by John McPhee
   - Discussion of requirements for radar detection: materials, location, activity of vessels
   - Review of the summaries written on earlier discussions: navigation aids, wind speeds
   - Reflection written on the realization of the limits of men and mechanics against the sea
   - Discussion of safety measures invented to allow successful work and exploration in the ocean environment
   - Identification of the need for constant vigilance, careful planning, and assessment near and on the sea

6. Essay Genre: Individual Oral Report

   LEARNER CONNECTION: Interesting sea-related experience
   - Discussing interests and experiences extemporaneously with associates
   - Identification of an interesting experience
   - Adding complexity by reading two quotations, examples of experiences by a current American essayist and a contemporary American essayist:
     (1) Sea stories by McPhee (anecdote)
     (2) Autobiographical boats by E. B. White in his essay, "The Sea and the Wind That Blows" (complete report)
   - Writing a one-sentence summary of each selection
   - Using metacognition to plan, monitor, and evaluate student knowledge
   - Writing a reflection on the experience chosen for the report
   - Clarifying details as necessary through research
   - Writing an outline or notes on notecards or other efficient methods

CHAPTER 4

7. Essay genre: Compare and Contrast

   LEARNER CONNECTION: The college's ship, tugboat, and wooden sailboat
   - Identification of the college tugboat's, sailboat's, and ship's characteristics
   - Providing complexity with a quote on connotations of the word "ship" by John Fowles from his book *Shipwreck*
   - Brainstorming and listing data on the college's 500-foot training ship
   - Brainstorming and listing data on the college's eighty-eight-foot wooden sailboat
   - Brainstorming and listing data on the college's seventy-six-foot steel tugboat
   - Review of data included: dimensions, materials, propulsion, communications, safety, educational potential

8. Essay genre: Cause and Effect

   LEARNER CONNECTION: Tide tables
   - Reading tide tables: printed tables with times of pre-calculated low and high tides for an area
   - Reviewing how the moon's gravity affects the oceans and causes the low (ebb) and high tides; occurring at approximately twelve-hour intervals
   - Reviewing how the sun's weaker gravitational influence, causes the very low (neap) and highest (spring) tides
   - Providing complexity with the quotation by Samuel Eliot Morison from *Spring Tides:* "Their predictability explains why tides are the sailor's friend."
   - Linking how tides affect marine experiences on and near the water
   - Writing a reflection about the tidal cause and effect when living by the sea

CHAPTER 4

9. Essay Genre: Group Oral Report, using the cause-and-effect genre

   LEARNER CONNECTION: Maritime college activities on the North Atlantic Ocean
   - Review of maritime-related knowledge: the training ship, the historic sailing vessel, pirates, extreme weather, navigation
   - Identification of writing ability selects the captains, first mates, crew
   - Defining of the roles and duties of captains (group leaders,) first mates (second-in-command,) and crew (remainder of class)
   - Brainstorming the aspects of topics by captains
   - Increasing complexity by providing the root and meaning of each aspect's term in the report introduction: propulsion, weapon, extreme weather, navigation, tall ships
   - Review and research of extreme weather found in the North Atlantic
   - Aspect linking cause: ocean's shallowness; and effect: winds develop and cause extreme weather
   - Review and research of the 500-foot training ship
   - Aspect linking cause: propulsion; and effect: moving on water
   - Review and research of modern pirates
   - Aspect linking cause: piracy; and effect: weapons used
   - Review and research of sailing tall ships
   - Aspect linking cause: ship size and sail area; and effect: amount and types of sails rigged for moving
   - Review and research of navigation
   - Aspect linking cause: exploration and safety at sea; and effect: history of navigational aids
   - Notes on research according to captains

10. Essay genre: Persuasion

   LEARNER CONNECTION: R/V Friendship, the college's fourty-eight-foot steel research vessel
   - Adding complexity through Carl Safina's quote using deductive reasoning: "Water invented animals to move itself around"
   - Sea research and exploration on the R/V Friendship
   - Linking maritime facts, add others:
     (1) Length of the US coastline is 12,380 miles, twelfth longest in the world
     (2) Length of Maine's coastline is 3,478 miles, fourth longest in the United States (Alaska, Louisiana, and Florida are longer)
     (3) Ninety-five percent of the world's goods travel by water
     (4) More than 75 percent of the world's population lives on the coasts
     (5) Facts connected to R/V Friendship's exploration
   - Reflection written on research or knowledge of a marine-related fact or problem

CHAPTER 4

11. Essay genre: Argument

   LEARNER CONNECTION: The sea's importance
   - Add complexity through Charles Darwin's quote on "The illimitable ocean"
   - Acknowledge the college's maritime collection of literature, authors, and research about the sea
   - Identification of the significance of maritime information through college(s) dedicated to the knowledge, research, training, and certification of mariners
   - Read quote "The sea is a sanctuary," by Maine naturalist Harry Goodridge from his memoir *Andre the Seal*
   - Definition of sanctuary: for marine life, human recreation, and exploration, safety at sea during a storm
   - Brainstorm the sea's resources
   - Definition of claim: a value, policy, or fact
   - Identification of Goodridge's claim: value
   - Definition of warrant: a belief, principle, or assumption
   - Identification of Goodridge's warrant: belief
   - Identification of evidence and criteria
   - Reviewing the aspects of Goodridge's claim of the sea as a sanctuary

EXPLORATORY WRITING THINKING EXERCISES TEMPLATE

Use the form below to provide the Learner Connection from student experience. Provide a Complexity Quote from a literary or other source to expand thinking and offer reflection. Exploratory Writing is a productive method to initiate thinking, create perceptions, supply a base for further instruction, and prepare for Formal Writing. See the next page for an example.

1. What is the Learner Connection for Exploratory Writing in the genre of _____ ?
2. What Complexity Quote will introduce related thinking?

3. Which exploratory forms are applicable in your discipline/content area? Select possibilities from the Exploratory Writing Forms list; add others as needed.

_____

_____

_____

_____

CHAPTER 4

EXAMPLE OF PLANNING EXPLORATORY WRITING

1. What is the Learner Connection for Exploratory Writing in the genre of description?
   A ship's log
2. What Complexity Quote will introduce related thinking?
   Reading a quote on logbooks by John McPhee. Information included in a ship's log: date, time, speed in knots, weather, personnel, events of the voyage, circumstances, and surroundings. Explain the historical origin and modern use, keepers of the log, importance for records of many kinds: insurance, engineering, scientific, and others.
3. Which Exploratory Writing forms are applicable in your discipline/content area? Select possibilities from the Exploratory Writing Forms list given; add others as needed.
   a. *Review—McPhee quote with information described above*
   b. *Reflection—learner's experience: keeping a log for reading, scouting, gas mileage, travel*
   c. *Aesthetics—observing the sea's color: blue*
   d. *Word exploration—roots for the words describing blue*
   e. *Listing—five synonyms for blue: azure, cerulean, cobalt, indigo, sapphire*

USING EXPLORATORY WRITING

Exploratory Writing is essential for developing thinking skills. In the process, original perceptions are discovered, becoming ideas, and leading to insights. Moreover, Exploratory Writing establishes a base for Formal Writing. Instruction for each genre in the Composition course presented literary selections as models, with essays written in class.

The Formal Writing forms most widely assigned across the curriculum are the essay, including essay exams, and the research paper, separately examined in chapters 5 and 6.

Exploratory Writing effectively inspires thinking across the curriculum, and is applicable in every discipline and on every level, as shown in chapters 8 and 9.

5

FORMAL WRITING PERSPECTIVES

Higher cognitive functions, such as analysis and synthesis, seem to develop most fully only with the support system of verbal language—particularly, it seems, of written language.

—Janet Emig, 1977

Thinking skills instruction creates completed ideas in the third thinking skills element. Formal Writing organizes Exploratory Writing ideas into a perspective, and provides a specific format for information and written expression. Formal Writing is an inclusive example of thinking skills, since the longest phase of thinking is involved, encompassing the writing process of drafts and revision. Formal Writing includes Independent Writing, discussed further in chapter 6.

Formal Writing emphasizes essays. The common academic writing form in every discipline is created from a perspective reflecting the rhetorical considerations of exploring an idea and its significance. The essay genres studied in the Composition course organizes knowledge from the learner's perspective. Not only the time involved, but also the format, contributes to the thinking process. Emig explains,

> A unique form of feedback, as well as reinforcement exists with writing, because information from the *process* is immediately and visibly available as that portion of the *product* already written. The importance for learning of a product in familiar and available medium for immediate, literal (that is, visual) rescanning, and review cannot perhaps be overstated.[1]

Across the curriculum, the essay (including exams) is the Formal Writing task most assigned. The essay genres taught in the Composition course are useful for thinking across the curriculum. Additionally, the genres provide a familiar method supplying writing guidelines. Other disciplinary writing forms, such as a lab report, are more specialized.

Original examples of the essay genres are written in class, after reading maritime literary selections as models or research data for material. Important writing, theories, and discoveries across the curriculum may similarly serve. Disciplines may also present an artifact, observation, data, equation, musical performance, film, or other source.

CREATING A THESIS

Assign a thinking activity, such as summarizing the selection, or writing a reflection to ensure comprehension by reviewing the ideas presented in the literary selections or data. Use the comments or analysis for possible thesis statements, or to guide original Formal Writing in the specific genre.

The thinking exercise is especially applicable for in-class writing, and is immediate preparation for formal responses. Expand reasoning about disciplinary content through description, process analysis, cause and effect, classification, division, compare and contrast, argument and persuasion, or narration.

The essay genres organize thinking, offering a perspective. Coordinating content and form, the genres are invaluable for clarification. Thinking skills from the genres are considered on the following pages.

CHAPTER 5

THINKING SKILLS IN FORMAL WRITING

Consider the implications of each genre:

- Why are the specifics given by cause and effect important?
- What will compare and contrast emphasize about a topic?
- Why analyze a process?
- What answers are provided when students divide topics?
- What will description writing show?
- How does classification assist knowing?
- What does a narration about a topic accomplish?
- What type of information is presented in an individual oral report?
- How can persuasion through deductive or inductive thinking influence reasoning?
- In what way in a group oral report is thinking extended?
- How can an argument based on a belief/principle/assumption be proved through developing a value/policy/fact?
- How can a combination of genres present information?

THINKING ABOUT CONTENT THROUGH WRITING IN A GENRE

Excluding exam essays, what disciplinary content will benefit from thinking and writing in an essay genre? Using the genres studied in the Composition course, content from any discipline may be the model, provide data, originate an inquiry or problem, and supply evidence in Formal Writing.

Valued most highly in thinking skills is Learner Insight. Original thinking about content, beginning with Exploratory

FORMAL WRITING PERSPECTIVES

Writing, is the basis of academic essays in any genre. The thesis, formed by an inquiry or problem and supported by the writer's reasoning and evidence, forms the Learner Perspective from critical thinking and analysis.

Thoughts on a subject are the basis and content of the essay, such as life measured by boats from E. B. White's essay "The Sea and the Wind That Blows," or sea-related geological background from John McPhee's "Travels of the Rock." The essays are interesting for the different perceptions presented; the range of topics is wide. Both essays have a sea-related perspective, yet each have a separate focus.

The Learner Connection to an academic subject is singular due to experience. Exploratory Writing connects with the experience and offers expansion by complexity and reflection. Formal Writing in various genres is guided by the excerpts or other examples and are models for a response.

Perceptions from the individual's perspective are the foundation for essays. Essays are assigned as thinking responses, using the genres as academic essays, in short papers, oral reports, or for essay exams.

Below are examples of thinking skills activities from Maritime Literature for student practice in writing summaries, finding a thesis, and modeling genre compositions. Following are the essay genres instructed in the Composition course, listed with thoughtful literary excerpts describing insightful topics. Also included are prompts for incorporating the genres across the curriculum.

CHAPTER 5

THINKING EXERCISES FOR FORMAL WRITING

1. Gather ideas from Exploratory Writing.
2. Read the literary excerpts modeling the genre, observe data, or other sources as an example.
3. Practice creating thesis statements or analyze writing topics from the example by writing a:
   - Summary
   - Brief: One-sentence/one-minute/one-paragraph summary
   - Guided summary: writing focused on a specific aspect
   - Reflection
   - Guided reflection: writing focused on a specific question

ADDITIONAL EXERCISES USING ESSAYS

The Composition course occasionally used a complete essay, rather than an excerpt, as a model for essay writing in a genre, or as information in an exam. A complete essay is additionally analyzed for content, as essays contain diverse material, presented through the author's perspective, for thinking skills.

When an essay is used as a genre model, a guided summary or reflection is written as an analytical exercise, highlighting an important aspect of the essay. In an exam, a question related to the content is asked. For more information on exams, see chapter 7.

Complete essays used from the Composition course are as follows:

1. "The Sea and the Wind That Blows"—E. B. White
   - Model for the oral report genre.
   - Sea related: thinking about experiences in boats.

2. "Travels of the Rock"—John McPhee
   - Literary selection for the midterm exam.
   - Uses many types of genre writing.
   - Sea-related: Plymouth Rock, geological, and historical concepts.
3. "Don't Say That about Maine"—Kenneth Roberts
   - Model for argument genre.
   - Uses many types of genre writing.
   - Sea-related: longitude; weather, building boats and ships, intellectual accomplishments.
4. Students review their summaries and reflections for thesis statements, topics, and direction.
5. Write an original essay example of the genre.
6. Write a short paper, or complete an essay exam.

CHAPTER 5

MARITIME LITERATURE EXAMPLES AND TOPICS

1. Writing genre: Description
   Literary examples:

   - The color of coastal and deep water—Rachel Carson (short)
   - Phosphorescence in the ocean—Charles Darwin (short)
   - "Plunging waves are the most impressive"—Willard Bascom (long)
   - Details of fine surf—Henry Beston (long)

   In your discipline, how can a literary selection, observation, or object prompt a descriptive essay?

2. Writing genre: Narration

- Mathematical measurement of the height of a 112-foot wave by the length of a ship—Rachel Carson (short)
- "My favorite spring high [tide] on the rocky Maine coast comes in May."—Samuel Eliot Morison (short)
- Sighting a bluefin tuna—by Carl Safina (long)
- Nathaniel Bowditch's influence on navigation—John McPhee (long)

In your discipline, how can a narrative essay explain a learner's thought process?

CHAPTER 5

3. Writing genre: Division

- Division of the day by times of watches stood aboard ship—Richard Henry Dana
- Two kinds of scientific discovery thrills, one planned, another by chance—William Beebe

In your discipline, how can a division essay introduce description?

4. Writing genre: Classification

- Ocean meteorology and winds—Captain Joshua Slocum
- Types of plankton found in seawater—William Beebe

In your discipline, how can a classification essay assist a learner's comprehension?

CHAPTER 5

5. Writing genre: Process Analysis

- Training a third mate aboard ship—Skip Strong (short)
- Changing burners in a steam turbine—Skip Strong (short)
- Nautical astronomy—Captain William Slocum (long)
- How a wave breaks—Willard Bascom (long)

In your discipline, how does a process essay explain an important activity?

6. Speaking/writing genre: Individual Oral Report

   (1) "Did you sail bosun with Columbus?" is a familiar quip when sharing sea stories with a long winded sailor (Anecdote)
   (2) Autobiographical boats by E. B. White in his essay "The Sea and the Wind That Blows" (complete report)

Anecdotes may inspire, provide evidence, and enliven an oral report; how are they useful in other ways?

Why is an oral report a primary source for research?

CHAPTER 5

7. Writing genre: Compare and Contrast

- Comparison of the usage of tugboats and ships—Skip Strong (short)
- Comparison of the animals living in the sea and on land—William Beebe (short)
- Comparison of a tugboat and a sailboat—Joseph Conrad (long)
- Comparison of microscopic and gigantic sea organisms—William Beebe (long)

In the history of your discipline, how can an early theory and a modern theory be compared and contrasted to show how a long-standing problem was solved?

8. Writing genre: Cause and Effect

   - Force of waves causing environmental changes— Rachel Carson
   - A book written by a naturalist's father unintentionally causes the public to devastate tidal pools— Edmund Gosse

In your discipline, assign a cause-and-effect essay to show a beneficial result from:

(A) Active research and observation
(B) Reading and thinking

CHAPTER 5

9. Speaking/writing genre: Group Oral Report, using the cause-and-effect genre

   - Sea-related topic for research: T/S State of Maine, pirates, tall ships, navigation, extreme weather—assigned by instructor
   - Aspect chosen by the captain or group leader of cause and effect: propulsion, weapons, sailing methods, history, North Atlantic, respectively

In your discipline, assign a group oral report to inform the class and explain why specific theories or documents are important.

10. Writing genre: Persuasion

- "The beauty of a two day old seal pup"—Harry Goodridge (short)
- Achievements, including improving sea education, and the thoughtful personality of American Commodore Perry—Samuel Eliot Morison (short)
- "A great mind is a good sailor"—Ralph Waldo Emerson (long)
- "If an Englishman wishes to have such a patriotic feeling, it must be about the sea."—Robert Louis Stevenson (long)

In your discipline, assign a persuasion essay to convince students that writing assists thinking.

CHAPTER 5

11. Writing genre: Argument

- "While the ocean may look the same as it has for millennia, it has changed, and changed greatly."—Carl Safina (belief)
- "That was the kind of recognition that had meaning to the salvage men. It was the only kind they ever cared about."—Farley Mowat (principle)
- "*Don't Say That about Maine!*" essay refuting the assumption that Maine only produces watermen and woodsmen since it is located in the northern latitudes, where it is too cold to produce intellectual activity.—Kenneth Roberts (assumption)

In your discipline, assign an argumentative essay on a controversial problem involving water in the student's home state.

Aesthetic components guide the Composition course. The sea's appearance and characteristics arouse a response. Inspiration from an individual's reaction colors thinking, since the brain is affected by emotions and motivation, acknowledged earlier in chapter 1.

Classic Maritime Literature selections are beautifully composed, and describe striking background content, as well as memorable examples for genre models. The third thinking skills element of Formal Writing provides an aesthetic, as well as other perspectives, applicable across the curriculum.

When writing using a form of rhetorical thinking in the genre best suited to the material, reasoning increases. Ideas and perspectives result in in-depth thinking about content. For example, comparing and contrasting the attributes of marine species help emphasize specific differences. Learners should be competent in the writing forms, able to choose appropriately, and write using the genre's characteristics.

Essays using information from the student's major is the primary function in the Essay Series and exams. All the writing genres listed, as well as other writing forms specific to a discipline, may apply the process. By transferring thinking skills to other disciplines, the learning activities demonstrate that writing is compatible and enhances any area of study. Chapter 8 explores writing in other disciplines.

Completed thinking in Formal Writing is thinking practice for research papers. The ultimate thinking assignment, replacing the final essay exam, is Independent Writing. Discussed in chapter 6, an Independent Writing assignment is the final evaluation preferable for thinking instruction through writing.

6

ULTIMATE THINKING
Independent Writing

> *Help students to realize that the main purpose of their education is to develop their intellect ... they can produce their own ideas, not merely reproduce someone else's ideas.*
> —Arthur Costa, 1987

The Composition course requires extensive original writing in the final assignment. Independent Writing is the culmination of thinking skills instruction. The last thinking skills element combines the preceding three elements in a comprehensive project expressing Learner Generated Inquiry, reasoned evidence, and conclusive insight on a nautical subject.

The most logical method for increasing thinking through writing is the Independent Writing assignment. The best thinking opportunities require a Learner Generated Inquiry or a perceived problem. The assignment includes self-monitoring, evaluation, planning, and significant time and support for creating. When offering new knowledge, or information viewed from a new perspective developed with focused thinking in Independent Writing, learner insight is the goal is Learner Insight.

CHAPTER 6

As Fulwiler claims,

> Such papers ask students to perform a variety of significant intellectual tasks, both conceptual and rhetorical . . . they become better thinkers and communicators . . . learn higher-order thinking skills that will color the way they receive, process, formulate and communicate ideas the rest of their lives... at the heart of this process rests the research assignment.[1]

Instruction for writing the research paper allocates time for completing preliminary thinking, reading, and writing for effective reasoning and perception. Presenting independent analysis to show in-depth comprehension is essential. Easily tracing the reasoning in a paper is an important factor in assessment.

Successful thinking is expressed through logical reasoning and offers an original perspective. Concluding the thought process, a final statement highlights insight. Furthermore, Independent Writing is the forum for academic progress, in thinking skills instruction, and in advanced research and development across the curriculum.

The long paper is the highest order of content reasoning and creativity. Accordingly, the assignment offers the highest assessment value, indicative of the accomplishment in thinking through writing in the Composition course. Twenty grade points are offered for ideal completion. A significant number of papers submitted received the distinction.

THINKING PREPARATION FOR WRITING

Throughout the course, from the announcement and details in the initial class; recharging at midterm with key resource accessibility including a seminar, individual conferences, and prospectus review; followed by specific written components submitted at well-planned intervals between midterm and the last class meeting; thinking is prominent.

Moreover, the final assignment in each genre of short papers, as well as the complex Essay Series, supplies practice for the fourth thinking skills element. Independent Writing, in a variety of formats, is the focal activity concluding study of every genre in Composition.

Instruction in the Composition course prepares for the independent project through:

- Attentive scheduling of each learning activity for writing the long paper.
- The midterm research seminar defining and locating resources by the director at the college Resource Center, with time for individual familiarization of the center.
- A preliminary individual conference discussing a written or verbal prospectus and additional conferences as needed.
- Exploratory Writing for topic and title selection, creating the Learner Generated Inquiry.
- Focused thinking to summarize a chosen topic.
- A thesis statement reflecting the Learner Generated Inquiry.
- Selecting relevant resources for evidence.
- Importance of primary sources.
- Examining an assortment of secondary sources.
- Limits of electronic research to databases.
- Elimination of websites for possible use as a source; if used, do so with discretion and verification.
- Applying metacognition when writing, analyzing, and evaluating.
- The significance, review, and practice of appropriate documentation.
- Knowledge and practice of the writing process with drafts and revising.

CHAPTER 6

- Submission of a paper answering the Learner Generated Inquiry.
- Demonstrating insight in thinking and creating new knowledge, or a new perspective.
- Reinforcing thinking skills, the procedures are useful in every discipline.

Writing and literature professor John C. Bean suggests the following additional activities:

1. "Assign a formal exploratory essay as an intermediate stage in a research project . . . the subject matter of the essay is *the student's thinking process*, the essay encourages and rewards critical thinking, while giving teachers wonderful insights into the intellectual lives (and study habits) of their students."[2]
2. Request that "all writing associated with the paper, from lists of resources to 'doodles' be submitted with the final draft,"[3] specifically discouraging plagiarism.

EXPLORATORY WRITING: THE LEARNER GENERATED INQUIRY

Independent Writing in a research paper revitalizes a form well founded for expressing perceptions, and remains pertinent for thinking skills instruction. Curiosity prompting academic inquiry is undiminished. In writing to learn for an extended period, reasoning is propelled by individual interest—the Learner Generated Inquiry.

Although a single research paper in a basic writing course may be insufficient to completely demonstrate advanced reasoning, in-depth use of primary sources, and acknowledging important content in more than one discipline, the long paper substantiates thinking through writing. Components are applicable to advanced projects, and exercise ability for independent inquiry and writing in other disciplines.

In the Composition course, the Independent Writing assignment is based on a Learner Generated Inquiry, a student's question or problem about anything related to the sea, including the course. Through thinking and writing on maritime topics in the genres, a perspective is acquired.

In the process, learners will encounter an inquiry related to any aspect. For example, how did a fully loaded supertanker become the only ship available to rescue the tug and space shuttle's barge? How does Polaris complicate navigational calculations? Is every third, seventh, or tenth wave larger? How are ancient marine life forms: the shark, jellyfish, and horseshoe crab capable of improving human health? Why is spartina nutritionally important?

Any marine topic: safety or starfish regeneration, Tennyson or trout, water turbines or wave dynamics, is open for speculation. Similar expansive reasoning in any discipline is to be encouraged. Thinking is apprised as a voyage of discovery.

In his 2004 book, *What the Best College Teachers Do*, educational researcher Ken Bain observes that "intriguing, beautiful or highly important problems, authentic tasks that challenge them to grapple with ideas, rethink their assumptions, and examine their mental models of reality,"[4] are presented by successful college teachers.

Such problems are part of thinking skills instruction in the Composition course, and the Learner Generated Inquiry engages students specifically in Independent Writing. Furthermore, exploration is vital in all disciplines.

In an Independent Writing assignment, students first apply thinking skills for self-direction. Exploring a topic appealing to the learner inspires innovation. The self-directed inquiry provides a perspective to guide the answer, and is additionally directed from the perceptions found. Moreover, Fulwiler maintains, a student's "very best resource is their own curiosity and persistence, their willingness to ask questions . . . to find good answers."[5]

THESIS-GUIDED FORMAL WRITING

Initial thinking about the Learner Generated Inquiry is expanded by Exploratory Writing. Exploratory Writing forms open and offer ideas. Focus is additionally determined through assessing what is found, exploring the directions possible for the answer. Choosing the ideas that answer the inquiry in an interesting direction also suggests the title of the paper.

Forming a Thesis

Selecting the paper's direction through important perceptions forms a perspective. The viewpoint will coordinate ideas and pinpoint a thesis. Stating the thesis through a carefully worded title coordinates interest and response. Introducing the topic and direction through the thesis, which initiates the answer to the Learner Generated Inquiry, predetermines the paper's content.

Formulated from the Learner Generated Inquiry, the thesis clarifies the course of thinking and writing. Leading critical thinking, the focus of the paper expands the response.

From the Composition course, intriguing examples are as follows:

- Inquiry about oil rigs specifying the unique aspects of the structure.

- Asserting that a ship's pilot is the zenith of nautical expertise through interviews with pilots supplying detailed experience.
- Proving the importance of the modern Merchant Marine considers world economics, notably shipbuilding and related industries.
- Interpreting the importance of underutilized fish species for food as only a myth, since all species are overfished, inadvertently destroyed as bycatch, or become food replacements for other marine life.
- The diverse methods of desalination that may supply the answer to the world's water shortage.
- A mathematical formula is created to explain how a sail works, according to the laws of physics.

Presenting Evidence

Thinking about the significance of the topic leads to the main section of the paper. The body of the paper examines and clarifies the points surrounding and investigating the inquiry. Reasoning maintains interest and seeks proof through research.

Discussing and exploring relevant indicators are affected by the resources chosen. Primary and secondary sources have specialized strengths.

Primary Research Sources

The power of primary resources, offering original information from interviews, questionnaires, or surveys is originality and freshness, both in content and language, spoken and recorded.

Plan specific questions, and seek responses that validate the thesis. Provide time and space for individual commentary.

CHAPTER 6

Such allowances for digression can provide details, examples, and quotes; distinctive support for the viewpoint to be proffered.

Actual examples, supplied by precise quotes, provide reasoning and create insight. Thinking and reflecting about the thoughts of an author as stated in an interview offer ideas and originality seen in the models inspiring writing in the Composition course, from the literary selections to the quotes in the Essay Series. See an excellent example in chapter 9 from Chuck Paine's words concerning aesthetics.

Secondary Research Sources

Information from secondary sources solidifies the thesis. Select pertinent writings from original works and essays, memoirs and autobiographies, updated material, and reported interviews. Examine specifics, and choose knowledge referring closely to original information. Reviews of authors and their work are preferable to general references (unless necessary for background, such as dictionary definitions) and electronic sources.

Carefully assess the material used. For the Composition course, electronic sources are allowed only as databases. Student use of websites and other electronic information is discretionary and subject to extensive verification. Until the vast range of all writing is transferred unabridged to an electronic "library," a previously selected assortment of information is a questionable and limited resource to be assessed and so noted.

Correct Documentation

Documentation must be similarly reviewed. Users should become aware of the significance of noting as a disciplinary evaluation. The notation style is according to identifiable details of resources. In documenting research in writing and literature, the Modern Language Association (MLA) style is used; knowledge of authors are valuable, so complete names are stated first. However, an instructor should advise, and also update the preferred format as needed.

In the social sciences, for example, the time frame must be readily available to a reader. Chronological order is significant in research, so the date is entered after the author(s) in the American Psychological Association (APA), style. Other formats, such as the Chicago Manual of Style (CMS), the Council of Science Editors (CSE), and the American Mathematical Society (AMS), similarly position features important in the field for readers' further inquiries. Additionally, documentation may vary for publishing, news, and business; seek advice on which format is required.

The research paper becomes part of the ongoing knowledge in a discipline. Therefore, correctly documenting sources both acknowledges the work of others, as well as locates relevant information.

Clarity

Simplify not only the diction of the paper, but also the description of evidence. Language in the present tense with active verbs helps follow the direction of reasoning and enlivens discussion. Select only supportive issues that are formed by concrete evidence and illustrated with specific details to prove the logic of the response.

Reinforcing the thesis, and retaining interest, precision in word choice and relevant examples support theories and insight. Contrary views, however, should also challenge important concepts and acknowledge the differences, eventually aligning with the central thesis, proving its strength.

CHAPTER 6

CONCLUDING STATEMENTS

Rhetorical thinking expresses meaning, forming a logical conclusion. Thinking skills are fully developed in the assignment. Bean writes "Teaching the thinking processes that underlie academic inquiry ... is a way of discovering, making, and communicating meanings that are significant, interesting, and challenging."[6]

Whether it creates or refreshes knowledge, the conclusion is an analysis of the thought process. Components complementary to the response of the Learner Generated Inquiry should be reiterated. Reasoning should be apparent, leading to final references summarizing original thinking. A brief synopsis of the content according to the insight may be made. Concluding the paper is an imaginative statement reaffirming its discoveries.

In a faculty survey on Independent Writing assessment at the maritime college, professor of engineering Peter Sarnacki exhorts:

> Begin your paper with a title page and introduction. Tell me where we will be going with the subject and capture my interest. Also, I will be looking for a good summary and conclusion! Do not tell me something of interest and then drop me without a good prediction or conclusion to all your hard work.[7]

Increasing thinking through increasing writing verifies that a long paper is preferable to an essay exam as a final evaluation. However, offering an essay exam as an alternate preliminary thinking exercise is stimulating. A modified version of a final exam using passages from Conrad's essay in his book, *The Mirror of the Sea* was given in the Composition course.

Exam level queries are ideal for practicing critical thinking. While instructors may decry the use of carefully crafted or traditional exam questions for practice, the questions impel independent thinking. Further discussions of exams as final evaluations are in chapter 7.

When writing independently, active learning discourages plagiarism. Knowledge important to the learner predisposes thinking about what is found through research to supplement the discussion of the thesis; asserting ownership of ideas, and projecting a "voice." Bean's suggestion for an exploratory narrative essay assignment about creating the paper is valuable for this aspect.

Furthermore, the antidote for plagiarism is knowing the writing "voice" of students, a specific benefit of in-class writing, exploratory and formal. Increasing writing for thinking and learning instruction obliges the instructor to recognize individuality; indeed, it cannot be ignored.

The thinking skills introduced and practiced through Independent Writing in the Composition course helps students direct, reason, and compose. Offering new information and ideas through learner insight and independent thinking, the research paper exemplifies proficient thinking through writing. Yale writing professor William Zinsser asserts: "The race in writing is not to the swift, but to the original."[8]

An Independent Writing project proffers ongoing metacognition, reflecting the first exercise on writing ability assigned in Composition. The Learner Generated Inquiry guides the project. Emphasizing thinking through writing is the goal of the course.

Evaluating individual writing ability in the first writing assignment of the Composition course, and successful accomplishment demonstrated in the final assignment coordinates course content, further illustrating thinking across the curriculum through writing.

7

PROACTIVE ASSESSMENT

Don't stress mistakes. Don't reinforce neuronal networks that are not useful.

—James E. Zull, 2002

Positive correction, with suggestions directing improvement, is most useful in thinking skills instruction. Supportive assessment for individual learning of higher-order concerns is fundamental for thinking development.

Nevertheless, the author once made an emphatic correction regarding a lower-order concern on a student's paper. Initial corrections included the explanation of irregular verbs; however, the student continued misspelling, presumably from habit, prompting this response:

> "Henceforth, _____! The correct spelling is 'writing,' NOT 'writting.'"

Notwithstanding the above lapse, corrections should be helpful responses, focused on revision, instead of editing.

CHAPTER 7

Since frequent, well-planned writing assignments will lead to better thinking and fewer mistakes, assign in-class writing on content material. Exploratory Writing for perception in a variety of forms, following with a formulated perspective in Formal Writing, and final evaluation through Independent Writing in a paper or exam is the usual sequence. However, using pertinent writing activities for thinking skills should be scheduled when most effective in a discipline.

LOWER-ORDER CONCERNS

Invariably, colleagues and critics will question the lack of emphasis on editing. Proofreading for grammar and spelling, as well as for composition errors, is necessary. In writing across the curriculum, thinking is the foundation, and sound writing the confirmation, so learners must be aware of the importance of presentation. Returning an assignment awash in correction marks highlighting every mistake, though, is discouraging and disorienting.

Therefore, when correcting, simply underlining lower-order mistakes is most effective. Other instructors suggest placing an x in the margin by the sentence containing the error. With either method, the student will self-correct, recalling and refreshing editing elements.

Lower-order incompetence should be improved through attendance at the college writing center (if one exists) a remedial course, or tutoring. Instructor time is ineffectual for attaining course goals if teaching emphasis is on previously learned (however incompletely) lower-order concerns. While thinking instruction encompasses reasoning on all levels of writing, higher-order concerns are the primary focus.

HIGHER-ORDER CONCERNS

"A policy of correctness in content is superior.... Correcting errors that directly affect meaning in the discipline gives students a better sense of why errors are important,"[1] maintains writing professor Stephen Tchudi. Assessment focuses on content, and writing conventions may be less emphasized. Furthermore, the majority of lower-order mistakes disappear when additional time is allowed for writing, or when multiple drafts are required.

ASSESSMENT CRITERIA

How well students achieve the objectives and goals of instruction are measured while grading. Student reasoning of content knowledge, expressed completely and insightfully in an appropriate form shows disciplinary awareness. Lack of terminology use, reasoning, and original insight display lower levels of comprehension. When assessing, it is important to note what comprises:

1. Important content knowledge
2. Acceptable reasoning
3. Awareness of disciplinary concepts
4. Exploratory Writing ideas
5. Formal Writing perspective
6. The final disciplinary evaluation: Independent Writing in a paper or an essay exam
7. Research paper insights
8. Thorough exam responses
9. Clear and concise writing
10. Which student responses receive the highest grade, and why

CHAPTER 7

Other disciplinary specifics should also be noted.

Instructors may compose a rubric, or prepare a list of attributes necessary for awarding letter grades representing the proportional percent of success. When grading, observe the requirements described for each level.

In the aforementioned report analyzing an engineering faculty survey on assessment at the maritime college, professor of engineering Peter Sarnaki submitted a detailed assessment rubric. Created to evaluate Independent Writing in the research project, the rubric is available to his students, as used in his course.

The first page of Sarnaki's rubric contains sections for evaluating language and form. A list of points deleted for missing writing specifics, including: inadequate length, title page, introduction, conclusion, footnotes, reference page, and lower-order concerns is on the second page. Below is the first page of his rubric:

> Rubric for evaluating the style and form of the gas turbines research paper:
>
> 1. Structure
>   - Organization
>   - Depth
>   - Emphasis
>   - Transitions into sections
> 2. Language
>   - Targeting of audience
>   - Clarity of sentences
>   - Connections between sentences
>   - Energy: strong verbs, conciseness
> 3. Illustrations
>   - Choice and design
>   - Introduction and explanation

- Labeling and placement
- Credits
4. Form
   - Format: layout, title page, introduction, and conclusion
   - Grammar: spelling and structure
   - Punctuation
   - Usage: affect/effect, verb tense, pronouns

Specific Comments:_____[2]

Note that Sarnaki allows for explicit instructor response in his final heading of "Specific Comments," and also leaves space for individual error in a category titled "GKW" in the "Term Paper Guidelines"[3] on the rubric's second page. Quoted earlier from chapter 5 is his sound advice for a strong conclusion to the Independent Writing assignment.

Primary Traits Analysis

Attribute-specific, also known as primary traits analysis, for thinking skills and writing assessment is precise. Used in the Composition course, the method's components specify details and clarify contrasts in assignments.

Rubrics are useful, as shown above, for particular assignments. Holistic scoring and general descriptive assessment, although simpler, rely on concepts that an instructor may internalize, thereby making them unapparent or widely varying. This assessment method may not be as accurate for various writing formats and disciplinary content.

Grading Points

Allocate grading points for the assignment's importance in the course total. Listed in the syllabus are the evaluation points for the Composition course assignments.

CHAPTER 7

The final evaluation is the Independent Writing project. Significant for the course's overall grade, Independent Writing is awarded the highest assessment in the point system, a possible overall grade transformation of twenty points. More details are in the previous chapter.

Creating Similar Assessment Criteria across the Curriculum

Research shows discrepancy in assessment, often by individual instructors in the same course, and inevitably in different disciplines. Instructors merit different writing styles, with diverse expectations. Instructors should provide their judging criteria for grading to students, preferably with an example. Models chosen for Formal Writing, therefore, should also illustrate desirable aspects. However, students should be able to submit an assignment, exam, or paper with reasonable expectations of similar criteria for appraisal across the curriculum.

Establishing positive criteria by thinking skills attributes exhibited through writing admits numerous approaches, and supports the importance of academic freedom. Considerations include:

- Desirable thinking skills
- Methods for encouraging thinking
- Recognition on all levels
- Individually appraised indications of awareness
- Disciplinary similarities
- Disciplinary differences
- Basic assessments for agreement

Learner Insight, seen as the goal for thinking skills, as well as creativity, is essential.

Thinking instruction develops important dynamics for evaluation. Elements of the process will support assessment criteria. Basic assessment may be ascribed, as appropriate in the fields of literature as in engineering. For example, clarity and originality are most often listed as desirable by the engineering faculty.[4] Such attributes are essential in both literature and engineering, and important in all other disciplines.

The following is the Composition course analysis, practical for disciplines across the curriculum.

CHAPTER 7

THINKING THROUGH WRITING ASSESSMENT

Listed below are factors considered in the Composition course, and for assessing writing in any discipline:

I. In order of importance:
  1. Is a thesis present?
  2. Does the thesis respond to the question?
  3. Is content guided by the thesis?
  4. Does the evidence contain supporting examples with details?
  5. Is the research thorough and applicable?
  6. Are quotations enhancing clarity and perception appropriately inserted?
  7. Is the response original, showing insight, and using a "voice" fitting the learner?
  8. What is notable?
  9. Is the answer complete?
  10. Are any basic writing conventions missing?

II. Specifically praise:
  - Originality
  - New insight or perspective
  - Interesting perceptions
  - Clear reasoning
  - Positive direction
  - Thoughtful organization
  - Components of good writing

III. Positive suggestions for correction include:
  - Recommendations for ongoing thinking
  - Directions for development
  - Applicable research sources
  - Additional theories

- Acknowledgment of strengths for improvement
- Correction for higher-order concerns
- Other proactive comments

IV. Final comments verifying the grade:
   1. Provide positive feedback
   2. Affirm all strengths of the paper
   3. Emphasize ideas
   4. Offer recommendations
   5. Focus on a few points for revision, rather than editing
   6. Correct only for higher-order concerns
   7. Are very specific
   8. Reinforce grading criteria

CHAPTER 7

EFFECTIVE CORRECTIONS AND COMMENTS SUPPORTING GRADING

Assign a grade to students' work reflecting the positive amount of strengths shown. Truthful comments from reading accompany the grade. The comments acknowledge successful elements and direct any needed thinking improvements.

Positive Comments

"Remember, recognition is a positive. It is constructive," writes Robert L. DeBruyn, in an article on increasing student achievement. "When recognition is used extensively in classes, academic achievement is enhanced.... Know that the most powerful recognition is for specifics.... The closer your recognition is to the effort and achievement of your student, the greater the impact and motivation."[5]

Review Sections II and III on the previous pages. For all disciplines, positive comments include:

- Acknowledging originality
- Goals achieved
- Interesting perceptions
- Positive suggestions
- Solid writing, including concision, clarity, thoughtful titles, explanatory introductions, directive topic sentences, appropriate transitions, well-expressed reasoning, and overall organization
- Corrections emphasizing higher-order concerns and specific disciplinary strengths

Neutral Comments

A lack of strengths is reflected by a lower grade, and accompanying neutral comments asking for clarification due to the missing components, for example:

- Is the thesis _____?
- How does the first paragraph describe _____?
- This is interesting; however, what is _____?
- This section is _____, as written.
- Some consideration of the research from _____ would be useful.
- How does _____ relate to _____?
- Could you give an example?
- Is a footnote needed to verify?
- When concluding, where does _____?
- Is _____ important for _____?
- This appears to be a first draft; rewrite.
- Details of disciplinary omissions.

If existing, mention any appropriate proactive appraisals. Add any other comments to direct improvement. This is the goal of all correction and grading: instructor responses regarding thinking and writing, directing improvement, and ensuring success. Calculus professor Dr. Marcia Birkin describes her methods:

> I do not grade informal writing, but I always respond to it. Here is where I learn the most about my students, and it is crucial that students feel their opinions, queries, or confusions are worthy of the professor's time and consideration. I do grade formal writing, in particular essay questions and technical reports. While the essay questions are usually graded for mathematical content over grammatical structure, the formal, transactional technical report is graded in three areas: mathematics, English, and analysis.[6]

CHAPTER 7

However, instructors can assist further. What techniques enable learners to improve for assessment?

THINKING IN EXAMS

Across the curriculum, essay exam questions are the most assigned examples of writing. Fulwiler believes the essay exam allows teachers to

> witness knowledge being processed ... see evidence of their students' reasoning ability ... promote learning ... asking students to consider new or imaginative combinations of knowledge.... So, while essays demand a lot of coordinated thinking and writing from students, making 'A' difficult to achieve, they also provide latitude: you can always find *something* approximate to say on an essay exam, and so seldom risk complete failure.[7]

The positive outcomes above uphold the use of essay exams. Moreover, as Fulwiler attests, several factors are considered in grading, providing several areas for exhibiting strengths. Occasionally, exams are the only writing assignment in a discipline. Thus, improving essay exam questions are requisite.

However, midterm and final exams, with a research paper assignment, are the usual forms of writing in most disciplines. Many instructors in the past envisioned writing to learn as consisting of only these forms. Answering questions in exams by combining content and rhetorical conventions was often the pinnacle of thinking skills. Furthermore, the prevalence of essay exams is a recurring example of thinking through writing.

While taking an exam, limited time does not allow dictionary use, widespread editing, and extensive revising.

Well-developed thinking skills from informal and Formal Writing assist thinking in exams. These should be incorporated in daily exercises, or assigned as opportunities to practice useful activities for writing exams, by:

1. Briefly freewriting or brainstorming, linking supportive evidence for a thesis.
2. Listing the main points supplying perspective for the answer, or writing a short outline.
3. Summarizing the ideas in one sentence to create the thesis.
4. Stating the thesis, or restating the question as a statement in the first sentence or paragraph.
5. Supporting the main point(s) of the thesis with logical evidence from examples with specific details.
6. Developing a perspective from the examples.
7. Concluding by combining the main points complementary to the restated thesis.

Further effective assistance is in exam information handouts, containing grading criteria, rubrics, and examples of successful answers. Moreover, reviewing typical questions, designating areas of importance to review, and discussing exam content in-class with groups are helpful. However, emphasizing thinking skills instruction activates content comprehension and logical reasoning.

COMPOSING ESSAY EXAMS

Nevertheless, instructors offer the most effective solution to ensure accurate thinking and response in exam writing: concise questions. Confusion regarding the instructor's intentions, vague comments, and widespread generalizations will be curtailed if an inquiry is incisive. Composing guidelines are simplicity and clarity—watchwords in Composition.

Essay Exam Question Examples

Address a single issue in depth, with clear instructions. In the Composition course, direct questions:

1. Request to prove/disprove.
   Example: Prove/disprove: All marine species benefit from a clean environment.
2. Evaluate by stating pros and cons.
   Example: Seen from space, light pollution almost dominates darkness on earth. What are the pros and cons of reducing light pollution?
3. Supply reasoning and evidence to agree/disagree.
   Example: Agree/disagree: Vigilance at sea is crucial.
4. Present a statement, ask why?
   Example I: Fishing regulations are successful for species biomass regeneration. Why?
   Example II: Why are fishing regulations successful for species biomass regeneration?
5. Use a single phrase to guide analysis of a topic.
   Example: According to Conrad, what attributes does the sea possess?

Review the exam questions from the Composition course at midterm and the last exam for additional examples. Simplicity in inquiry allows in-depth writing.

Students generally have questions, so allow time before the exam, and if necessary, during the administration, to clarify instructions and review directions. Therefore, a handout for the exam, with an example and details, is useful.

As advocated in Composition, if the expectation is built into the course, learners will be aware that questioning is an important part of thinking. Not only will the students' questions generally be well reasoned, but extensive thinking will also be encouraged.

Evaluate Exam Questions

As an instructor, read and write a response to the questions you have created, or ask a colleague to review. Evaluate the questions for:

- Simplicity
- Clarity
- Limited scope
- Specific guiding
- Avoidance of open-ended directives to analyze, create, or evaluate.

Thorough knowledge and sound reasoning are the objectives of essay exams. Precise inquiry is imperative for thoughtful responses.

In contrast, if your intention is to prompt creativity by offering an open-ended query, note that the process of writing is time consuming, and supply a single or reduced amount of concise exam questions. Whether the question simplifies focus on an important content matter, or is all inclusive to exemplify your intended course goal, ample time must be scheduled.

Ideal Evaluation for Thinking Skills Instruction

The logical method for increasing thinking through writing is the Independent Writing assignment. Successful thinking

CHAPTER 7

skills instruction inspires curiosity, elicits inquiry, and mandates originality, expressed most fully when writing independently. The importance of thinking in Independent Writing is significant for achieving direction for later research and development. Independent Writing projects are discussed in chapter 6.

An example acknowledging the worldwide importance of proactive thinking is the Nobel Prize, first offered in the disciplines of literature, physics, chemistry, economics, medicine, and for promoting peace in 1901. The prize for literature exemplifies the intention of the founder, Alfred Nobel, being writing for advancement in "an ideal direction."[8] Reflecting an association for positive reinforcement augmenting thinking, the prize offers distinction and support for Independent Writing in all genres.

Accordingly, Zull's observation from the chapter's beginning anchors grading and assessment in thinking skills instruction.

WRITING IN OTHER DISCIPLINES

> *Knowledge is not as compartmentalized as I thought it was. Writing is the key that opens the door.*
>
> —William Zinsser, 1990

Thinking skills applied in writing assignments are chosen for specific requirements in the discipline. Writing as a way of knowing is effective in any discipline. "Writing is an essential activity to create order . . . sense . . . meaning . . . as such, it is the heart of creative learning in both the arts and sciences,"[1] acknowledges Fulwiler.

Furthermore, "the mere process of writing is one of the most powerful tools we have for clarifying our own thinking. I am never so clear about a subject as when I have just finished writing about it," observes physicist James Van Allen. He adds, "The writing process produces that clarity."[2]

As Emig claims, "Scientists, artists, mathematicians, lawyers, engineers . . . 'think' with pen to paper, chalk to blackboard,

CHAPTER 8

hands on terminal keys ... developed thinking is seldom possible any other way."[3] She states that thinking in disciplines not based on linguistics nevertheless incorporates writing.

Fulwiler additionally stresses that writing is the foundation for thinking and

> learning knowledge *in all fields* as well as communicating that knowledge ... balance the curriculum as carefully with regard to writing as we currently do with reading activities. Few curricula recognize, implicitly or explicitly, that writing can have an equally important role in generating knowledge.... An individual's language is crucial in discovering, creating, and formulating ideas as well as communicating their substance to others.[4]

EXPLORATORY WRITING IN OTHER DISCIPLINES

As examined in chapter 4, Exploratory Writing in a range of forms is easily applied across the curriculum. The components of Preparatory Writing, discussed in chapter 3 is the base, and guides Exploratory Writing, also referred to as expressive or Informal Writing, beginning the thinking process. Select the form that best introduces or advances course content for the level of instruction.

For example, use a single question—such as the aforementioned inquiry about individual response to the sea in the Composition course; or one from the suggestions below to introduce instruction. Select an appropriate exploratory form for the response.

Another method is a series of questions, as mathematics professor Alan Marwine recommends:

One can always begin a course, and a journal, by asking students to write in response to questions like the following:

- What are your expectations for the course?
- What do you hope to learn?
- What do you want to accomplish?
- Why have you enrolled in the course?
- What are your first thoughts on _____ ?
- What are your first thoughts on _____ ?[5]

In addition, Marwine proposes another Exploratory Writing exercise and extension:

> If I were beginning a course in Euclid's Geometry, (based on a direct translation of Euclid) I would first ask a few of the aforementioned questions. When it came time for content, but prior to the students having done any reading, I would begin by asking them to write definitions for the following terms: point, line, straight line, and surface.
>
> Students will write definitions very different from Euclid's, so it would be useful to have them write a few words about such differences... read Euclid's definitions and react in writing to them: any reaction will do.... Anyone who uses writing in the classroom will have to confront the limits of time by establishing deadlines for each portion of an assignment.... I would want to allow time for a "What stood out for you?" question at the end of class.[6]

FORMAL WRITING PERSPECTIVES

In Formal Writing, the variety of essay genres available, practiced, and applied in the Composition course provide choices for coordinating content with form.

For example:

CHAPTER 8

1. Useful in the sciences, mathematics, and related disciplines
   - Cause-and-effect essays
   - Division
   - Classification
   - Description
   - Process analysis
   - Others
2. Effective in literature, history, and associated fields
   - Description
   - Narration
   - Comparison and contrast
   - Others
3. Widespread across the curriculum
   - Persuasion
   - Argument
   - Oral reports: individual, group
   - Discipline-specific writing forms

Writing may be assigned in many forms to develop thinking. For example, central to critical thinking is the summary. Analyzing any form of information, or used as an evaluation, a summary may be used to find a thesis, as well as state one; to guide the abstract of any lecture, report, or book; as the basis of persuasive writing, to conclude an argument or debate; and to complete the results of Independent Writing, exemplifying thinking on any topic.

The summary is an indispensable form for thinking through writing in every discipline. It is as essential for progress in learning as Independent Writing projects are for final evaluations.

Thinking activities through writing extend content knowledge. Use the four thinking skills elements as assignments for content interaction.

The Composition course follows the progression of Preparatory Writing, Exploratory Writing, Formal Writing, and Independent Writing when applying the thinking skills elements. While the method is most effective, decide how each element functions best in your discipline.

Writing is widely useful, though less prevalent in the arts, mathematics, and science. Emig describes the

> distinctions between (1) writing and all other verbal language processes—listening, reading, and especially talking; (2) writing, and all the other forms of composing . . . (3) composing in words and composing the two other major graphic symbol systems of mathematical equations and scientific formulae.[7]

Emphasizing writing, and how the thinking elements, including the essay genres and disciplinary writing forms, assist learning in nonlinguistically based disciplines are the focus of this chapter, as thinking and learning exercises for linguistic-based subjects have been earlier addressed. Thinking skills using writing, albeit in alternate forms, remains essential.

THINKING AND WRITING IN MUSIC EDUCATION

Thinking through Exploratory Writing to prepare is described by music education professor Carol W. Benton. She finds, "The overarching goal is to provide students with cognitive tools to become independent, lifelong music learners. The list of skills and components of metacognition appears to be a commonsense list of thinking habits used by excellent students in any educational setting."[8]

For example, Benton directs students to write an individual goal on a notecard, before beginning, for the musical activity in which they will participate. At the end of the activity, she instructs students to review the goal and evaluate what was achieved.[9]

As in the Composition course exercise assessing writing ability, music evaluation uses self-planning, monitoring, and evaluation. Richard Colwell states, "What we do know about thinking is that it is subject matter specific. Scholars think in a discipline: one thinks like a historian, or like a musician. The process of thinking is intertwined with the content of thought."[10]

Adds Benton: "Metacognition is . . . a type of thinking that helps students while they are engaged in learning tasks that are directly embedded in a specific discipline. . . . Although metacognition is applied in discipline specific learning, it does possess a transcendent, executive quality. It is the type of thinking whereby learners guide their intellectual efforts in any content area."[11] Moreover, she continues, "self-regulation is inherent in higher order thinking. . . . It may be argued that self-regulation is even more important in music learning than in other academic areas. Self-regulation is vital to success."[12]

To assist learning, the music exercise may be written frequently or daily for every practice session, rehearsal, or class, as well as for a performance. With the written reminder, students incorporate metacognition: examining, planning, and improving performance.

A written goal and the subsequent evaluation will focus learning, effective for music and other disciplines, performance-oriented or otherwise. Additional Exploratory Writing and thinking exercises Benton uses are as follows:

1. "Self-reflective writing, including journal writing, in response to a prompt provided by the instructor.[13]

A. The descriptive step: This is the music learning event (a practice session, rehearsal, performance, etc.).
B. The metacognitive step: These are thought processes that made learning possible for me.
C. The analysis step: These are the things that happened during the music learning event.
D. The evaluation step: These are the outcome of the musical event.
E. The reconstructive step: This is how I will make future music learning events better."[14]
2. "Self-assessment activities:
A. Strengths are identified, and evaluated in their musical progress.
B. Challenges are identified, with ideas for improvement planned.
C. Creating rubrics for evaluation.
D. Filling out practice, listening, and learning logs."[15]
3. "Working with a partner and thinking aloud to share learning activities. When required to explain their thinking process, students gained clarity and insight for solving problems."[16]

Concert pianist Orli Shaham emphasizes, "Classical music... has the potential to speak to everyone. This [is] music that is by its very nature both thought provoking and invites repeated listening."[17]

While the Composition class composed essays after reading exceptional Maritime Literature selections, aesthetics and modeling are equally, if not more, important in performance disciplines. Benton discovered that "listening to exemplary music performances enabled students to learn and perform as well as if they had practiced all day."[18]

CHAPTER 8

THINKING AND WRITING IN THE SCIENCES

In 2015, Professor of Science Education Dr. Michelle Smith of the University of Maine improved student comprehension of genetics with regard to their own health. Using this Learner Connection, Smith reinforced challenging genetic concepts several times, as:

1. An in-class question
2. Homework
3. Another question where students applied their knowledge to a new situation
4. An exam

Smith found that active learning, utilizing thinking techniques, increased student grades.[19] Her instruction corresponds to the four thinking skills elements of Preparatory Writing, Exploratory Writing, Formal Writing, and Independent Writing.

In another example using the thinking elements, physics instructor Mark S. Andrews instructs a unit on the nature of light. Below are the thinking and writing activities used, followed by listed thinking skills exercises.

THE NATURE OF LIGHT—M. S. ANDREWS

1. Preparatory Writing:
   A. Assigning a textbook chapter reading on the solar system, part of the Milky Way galaxy.
   B. Connecting content from the text with a quiz listing types of celestial bodies and probable material composition in the solar system.
   C. Lecture on differences between stars and planets, and the hierarchy of other objects in the universe.
   D. Updating discussions:
      - Former planet Pluto recently reclassified as a protoplanet
      - The asteroid belt between Mars and Jupiter, possibly a potential planet never formed due to Jupiter's very large gravitational field?
      - Saturn's rings are bits of rock and dust, possible remnants of the planet, or a destroyed or unformed moon?
      - Examples of comets, meteors, asteroids, dust, gases; other visible objects in the universe

2. Exploratory Writing
   A. Notes on the lecture
   B. Linking hypotheses, ideas, and comments from the discussions
   C. Learner Connection: observing the night sky with unaided eyes
   D. Adding complexity: visibility improvement
      - Telescopes—optical, radio, infrared; earth- or space-based
      - From the Hubble telescope, largest space-based optical in existence

CHAPTER 8

3. Formal Writing in one or several forms about how major objects in the universe are seen
   A. Summary: Why planets reflect available light
   B. Process essay: How stars produce light via fusion
   C. Reflection: The only star in the solar system: the sun
   D. Short paper: Comparing and contrasting a red giant star and a brown dwarf star

4. Independent Writing on the nature of light
   A. Thesis statement
   B. Characteristics of electromagnetic forces
   C. Light, as: Waves? Particles? Combinations? Alternating? Different forms?
   D. Evidence supporting a logical form(s) of light
   E. Learner insight developing the theory
   F. Conclusion restating thesis[20]

THINKING SKILLS EXERCISES FROM THE NATURE OF LIGHT

1. Begin with thinking Preparatory Writing:
   - Textbook reading assignment on the solar system
   - Quiz on the types and composition of celestial bodies
   - Lecture, notetaking, discussion, updates, and reasoning about objects in the universe
2. Continue with Exploratory Writing:
   - Learner Connection: night sky observation with unaided eyes
   - Adding complexity: increased visibility via telescopes of various powers and types
   - Visibility with the Hubble telescope
3. Organize thinking in Formal Writing:
   - Summary: visibility of planets
   - Process analysis essay: star visibility
   - Reflection: the sun
   - Short paper: compare and contrast: red giant star and brown dwarf star
4. The final evaluation in Independent Writing:
   - Thesis statement
   - Supporting evidence
   - Details and examples
   - Insight developing the theory
   - Conclusion complementary to ideas

CHAPTER 8

Andrew's curriculum uses thinking skills through Preparatory Writing, Exploratory Writing, Formal Writing, and Independent Writing to prepare, explore, and establish a perspective on what is known, and inquire further about the nature of light. Thinking through writing constructively directs content application in any discipline.

For actual observation and laboratory research, a more specific format for Independent Writing is used in the sciences. Sections required are:

1. Introduction
2. Methods
3. Results
4. Discussion
5. Conclusion
6. Recommendations

While the terminology is different, note the similarity to thesis-based writing. Especially important is reasoning in the Results (corresponding to the thesis-based Evidence) and suggested direction offered in Recommendations (the thesis-based paper combines Recommendations in one section of the Conclusion.)

"Scientific writing is a very highly organized and specialized form of writing, suited for the dissemination of results,"[21] states Alan Marwine. Both types are examples of insight—evaluative and creative thinking shown through Independent Writing.

In his curriculum design paper, "Curriculum Planning" Andrews asserts, "History is the thinking process of any discipline,"[22] summarizing how the progression of events and facts create background and support content.

Moreover, "Like every intellectual pursuit, physics has both a written and oral tradition. Intuitive modes of thought, inference by analogy, and other stratagems are used.... After creation is over, the results are recorded for posterity in a logically impeccable form,"[23] asserts physics professor William J. Mullins, at the University of Massachusetts. He concedes "Indeed, physics is based largely on analogy. For example, the ideas and mathematics of fluids are greatly similar to those in the theory of electromagnetic fields. If you understand a bit about nature's right hand, you ... know something about its left hand."[24]

Mullins teaches electricity and magnetism, as well as Writing in Physics, "a course that, while it has considerable physics content, also includes substantial amounts of writing ... to enhance and reinforce the subject being studied, not to teach grammar and spelling at the expense of the subject."[25]

THINKING AND WRITING IN MATHEMATICS

Stated earlier, notes in music are a means of writing, as are numbers in science and mathematics. Emig's "elegant summarizers" may be written as scientific formulae and mathematical equations. An established example, using algebra, is used in navigation.

Onboard, after taking a reading, apply the distance formula: $d = s \times t$ (distance equals speed multiplied by time) to later determine your location by "dead reckoning." Originating from the nautical reference to uncharted seas as "dead seas," or possibly from the term deduced (ded.) reckoning, the mathematical relationship provides a location when the skies are cloudy, and a sight cannot be taken.[26]

Even today, this method is practical, especially at dawn or dusk,[27] when electronics may be inconsistent, if insufficient satellites are aligned, or an energy source is unavailable. In the Composition course, a student created an equation in his Independent Writing project to analyze an aspect of sailing.

CHAPTER 8

Expressing the relationship of scientific concepts, or deriving the quadratic equation may initially be exploratory; however, learners show their depth of comprehension, and offer new ideas when they write. Learners will:

1. Begin reasoning and raise questions—in Preparatory Writing.
2. Explore problems and link concepts—in Exploratory Writing.
3. Explain their learning process—in reflections; the narration, oral and group report genres.
4. Give background information—using analogy; description, division, classification, compare and contrast genres and other genres of Formal Writing.
5. Describe the procedures or method—in process analysis, description, oral and group report genres.
6. Assess final results—in a summary; the description, cause and effect genres.
7. Develop a theory/compose an artwork/music/object—using the description, process analysis, persuasive and argumentation genres.

Marwine observes, "Mathematics has its own symbol systems, which, in their highest forms of expression, both pure and applied, permit the communication of ideas and expressions that defy precise verbalization."[28] Nevertheless, he advises,

> Informal writing exercises *do* permit teachers to become better guides, and even if they *only* encouraged students to identify their own problem areas, such exercises would enhance the quality of the student's understanding of the material. I submit that writing will do even more, but let us be content with these goals and reasons for incorporating writing into our classes.[29]

At Duke University, George D. Gopen and David A. Smith found that technological developments have rendered obsolete many techniques, such as extensive calculations, emphasized in their courses. Calculating and memorizing concepts had been previously stressed due to skills lacked by incoming students.[30]

So, Gopen and Smith incorporated "needing a new way to re-emphasize conceptualization in the mathematics curriculum ... [We use] the pedagogical efficacy of writing assignments, which require students to (re) articulate concepts before pushing the buttons. This new hope assumes that *thought* and *expression of thought* are so closely interrelated that to require the latter will engender the former."[31]

Furthermore, Gopen and Smith conclude:

> Several things are clear to us:
>
> 1. Mathematics teachers can incorporate writing assignments into their courses, with significant success and without unduly burdensome extra effort.
> 2. Thought and expression of thought are so inextricably intertwined that one cannot be good unless the other is as well.
> 3. Reader expectation theory succeeds in making better not only written products, but better writers.
> 4. Writing assignments can actually help students understand calculus.
>
> Perhaps most remarkable of all, the students, by their course evaluations, graded us an A for having added this writing component to their calculus course. Quoth one: Putting theory into words was—and still is—a challenge; but this helped me really *learn*, not just memorize, the concepts.[32]

An example, for an assignment presenting a mathematical word problem, to be explained through process analysis:

CHAPTER 8

Sailboats can actually go much faster when they sail across the wind. How so? Using what you have been learning in vector algebra, explain why sailboats can actually travel faster when the wind blows sideways [abeam] to their direction of travel, rather than from directly behind them.... Make your explanation clear.[33]

Students' thinking through writing can be examined for comprehension, and further assessed for accuracy. Moreover, instruction may be adjusted precisely. Additionally, the goals and objectives of the course consider the developmental needs of the class. It was also found that

> writing can serve other purposes as well. I've tried various techniques to motivate students in class, such as small group work, extra credit projects, and oral presentations. But I've always come back to writing assignments as the most successful way to involve students in the concepts they are studying... a personalized method of understanding the topic.[34]

Professor of Calculus Marian Birkin, a proponent of writing to teach mathematics at the Rochester Institute of Technology continues,

> I find writing generates an enthusiasm in the classroom, and changes students from passive thinkers to active thinker—participants. Most importantly, writing allows students to engage deeply in the content of a course in a way that tests and quizzes simply cannot, while providing a new form in which to engage discussion about their mathematical thinking, perception of the course, and interest in the subject. Writing can revive the bored students and provide less threatening activity for the student who is math anxious or has a lower skill level.
> For the strong math student, writing is a chance to show creativity. The same type of logical order is needed to work

WRITING IN OTHER DISCIPLINES

through a problem from statement to solution as is needed to construct a well-organized essay. Some features of essay writing include focusing a paragraph with a topic sentence, progressing through multiple paragraphs in a coherent thought pattern, and closing an essay with a summary statement. This parallels the formal process of a mathematical argument. Doing both simultaneously seems to reinforce the problem-solving process.[35]

In addition, she suggests an in-class writing exercise,

> applicable to any level of mathematics ... the student works with two sheets of paper, on which are posed the same problem at the top. On Sheet 1, the student writes mathematical steps to [a] solution, while on Sheet 2, she writes English sentences or phrases that correspond to the mathematical steps. Pairs of students, (who have different problems of the same type to solve) then exchange pages, and on a third piece of paper must follow their partner's English and convert sentences and phrases back to mathematical steps. At the end, partners compare answers, and usually discover the translation became garbled from the sender to the receiver. Rarely do answers agree, and it is the responsibility of the pair to decide where communication broke down.

The types of writing students may encounter during a quarter include some or all of the following:

- Short, in-class writings, usually expressive or informal
- Homework problems to interpret or analyze, or homework assignments calling for a reflection on a concept
- Essay questions on tests, and departmental final exams
- Formal technical transactional reports.[36]

To clarify the usefulness of writing, as earlier affirmed by Marwine, she concludes:

CHAPTER 8

I've learned a great about students' mathematical misconceptions, and I can usually pinpoint exactly where their thinking went wrong, and how to redirect it. Many students have told me they never thought about what they did, or why they did it while problem solving. Since writing requires the ability to communicate (if only to oneself) a process or an idea, most students comment that they have a deeper understanding, further clarity, and better retention of concepts after writing. Writing allows students to explore the constructs of a foreign language (mathematics) using a language in which most are fluent.[37]

Using writing to express thinking in science, mathematics, and the arts may use another system of notation, although words are still used in translation from these "languages." In-depth critical thinking is used to distinguish complex concepts from notes or numbers.

Used in professional thinking and writing, the methods are discussed in the next chapter.

WRITING ON OTHER EDUCATIONAL LEVELS

Learning is learning to think.
—John Dewey, 1938

The beginning of thinking coordinates with the beginning of writing. Attaining literacy allows methods of expression. The four elements of thinking through writing:

I. Preparatory Writing
II. Exploratory Writing
III. Formal Writing
IV. Independent Writing

are based on the thinking skills of writing. Emig describes writing as unique, due to its visual nature—synchronizing with the visual nature of the brain, according to Zull. Thinking through writing is the most effective approach for all levels of education.

CHAPTER 9

PRECOLLEGE EDUCATION

To this end, incorporating thinking skills in precollege education using Bloom's Taxonomy is advocated by English instructor Sally Leighton. After literacy is attained, she develops writing at the primary level by asking thinking questions in a range of assignments using the actual terms from Bloom's first three levels: remembering, understanding, and applying.

Advancing thinking and writing using Formal Writing in analyzing, evaluating, and creating begins in grade six, and continues in the secondary grades, by increasing complexity.[1]

However, Leighton has found that Formal Writing—notably the essay—has now been downgraded in importance on these levels, and replaced by the electronically based "I Search."[2] Nevertheless, an original essay remains part of the college preparatory assessment exams—the Scholastic Aptitude Tests (SATs), is a significant factor in college applications, and is integral to academic writing. The ideas forming perspectives for essays are discussed in chapter 5.

It is hoped that this change will be reconsidered. On the precollege level, introducing research, and practicing methods for exploration and selection are part of intellectual discovery. Source variety is of the highest importance in examining, thinking, and generating insight through research. Discovery promotes interest and stimulates thinking.

Teaching thinking skills will assist student reasoning in the required standardized tests in every area. Teachers who criticize "teaching to the test," may instead emphasize the skills. Creating curricula instructing thinking on a variety of topics and methods corroborates academic freedom.

This foundation enables thinking in writing to be incorporated across the curriculum. Thinking and writing as a way of knowing is universal. Practicing a customary method of exploratory, formal, and independent composition is effective and opens all disciplines. Leighton's methods are supported by C. B. Olson:

> Writing is the stage when thought is transferred into print.... All of Bloom's levels of thinking recapitulate the writing process.... the depth and clarity of thinking enhance the quality of writing, while at the same time, writing is a learning tool for heightening and refining thinking.[3]

Thinking through writing develops a learner's depth of engagement, as every discipline incorporates specific ways of thinking and learning. Furthermore, Emig suggests that there are

> certain features and strategies that characterize successful learning. These include the importance of the classical attributes of reinforcement and feedback. In most hypotheses, successful learning is also connective and selective. Additionally, it makes use of propositions, hypotheses, and other elegant summarizers. Finally, it is active, engaged, personal—more specifically, self-rhythmed in nature.[4]

Influential components include:

1. Disciplinary Language
   A. Terminology
   B. Vocabulary
2. History and background
   A. Events
   B. Discoveries
   C. Theories
   D. Hypotheses
   E. Formulae
   F. Equations

CHAPTER 9

   3. Resources
      A. Texts
      B. Supplementary: recommended, incidental
      C. Research: primary, secondary sources
   4. Instruction methods
      A. Writing
         (1) Thinking skills emphasis
         (2) Increasing complexity in assignments
         (3) Preparatory
         (4) Exploratory
         (5) Formal
         (6) Independent
      B. Reading
         (1) Models
         (2) Content
      C. Speaking
         (1) Asking thinking questions
         (2) Lecture
         (3) Discussion
         (4) Using directive terms
         (5) Instructor responses
   5. Assessment
      A. Objective evaluation
      B. Subjective evaluation
      C. Attribute-specific assessment
      D. Positive response and commentary
      E. Higher-order concerns
      F. Lower-order concerns
   6. Instructor
      A. Assets
      B. Writing
      C. Goals
      D. Objectives

7. Relation to other disciplines
   A. Arts
   B. Humanities
   C. Sciences
   D. Mathematics
   E. Professional
8. Other disciplinary aspects.

Writing is also the process best exhibiting thinking in learning. Bean maintains: "The most intensive and demanding tool for eliciting critical thinking is a well-designed writing assignment. Whatever the teacher's goals for a course, writing assignments can be designed to help meet them."[5]

The versatility of the summary as a critical thinking form has been previously acknowledged. The essay, including all the genres practiced in the Composition course, is similarly useful on every level of education.

Essay forms are not limited to any discipline. Knowing the forms available for writing across the curriculum offers a critical and creative choice for the writer, and for instructor planning. "I know I am successful as a teacher when students confess that they learned more from my writing assignments than from any other learning activity,"[6] affirms finance professor Dean Drenk.

Thinking activities through writing develop content. Use the thinking skills elements for content interaction. A summary of guidelines is reviewed on the next page.

CHAPTER 9

SUMMARY OF THINKING SKILLS ELEMENTS FOR INSTRUCTION

1. PREPARATORY WRITING

   Incorporate Learner Preknowledge and introduce courses or content by reading/recall, inquiry, evaluation and lecture/discussion, establishing background.

2. EXPLORATORY WRITING

   Establish the Learner Connection and add a Complexity Quote, encouraging original Learner Perception through content exploration.

3. FORMAL WRITING

   Organize Learner Perception from Exploratory Writing into a Learner Perspective to compose essays in various genres, short papers or other formal disciplinary assignments. Essay exams are valuable for faster, though limited, evaluation.

4. INDEPENDENT WRITING

   Learner Generated Inquiry independently investigates a topic further through research, and presents Learner Insight, offering new ideas or knowledge in a paper or project.

The progression is the method the Composition course follows when integrating the elements of the thinking skills. However, examine and assess each element, to see how the function is applicable for the level of instruction. How will the elements best exercise the objectives and achieve goals?

POSTCOLLEGE THINKING AND WRITING

In contrast to precollege instruction, postcollege educational goals accent professional achievement, usually fulfilling licensing requirements for professional practice. These fields include not only maritime positions, which require training, such as the Composition course to ensure adequate literacy for all levels of professionals through the STCW requirements, achieving experience through accumulating hours at sea, and completing examinations to assess knowledge.

Similar activities in other disciplines, including internships, practicums, and exams, in medical, veterinary, law, architecture, engineering, and other professions also require specific professional interaction and involve writing to communicate proficiency.

Illustrating the differences in disciplines, Emig describes the distinctions in thinking and composing in words, and "all the other forms of composing, such as composing a painting, a symphony, a dance, a film, a building."[7]

Moreover, observations leading from a tested hypothesis to a theory in the sciences, an idea composed, practiced, then performed creating art and music; or developed into an elegant yacht or distinctive architecture; or a problem solved by a solution producing an equation condensing a concept; corresponds to Independent Writing—the ultimate use of thinking skills.

The next page details adjustments showing alternate writing methods to apply thinking skills on the professional level of all disciplines.

CHAPTER 9

THINKING SKILLS ELEMENTS WITH ALTERNATE FORMS OF WRITING

1. PREPARATORY WRITING

   Preparation by experiences from reading, observing, or practicing brush strokes, musical scores, ballet movements, or computer-aided design (CAD).

2. EXPLORATORY WRITING

   Exploration in writing using language or alternate forms: musical notes, numbers.

3. FORMAL WRITING

   Formal compositions offering ideas in performance, results as equations, or other forms of evaluation in many professional fields, including exams.

4. INDEPENDENT WRITING

   Creation of new information, objects, or insight through independent research or design, composed in language or another method.

PROFESSIONAL THINKING AND WRITING

At the maritime college, an example of the importance of professional thinking and writing in engineering is described in Professor Stephen A. Collins's report, "Communications in Engineering." Information obtained from a faculty questionnaire and summarized in the report shows a "shift in the emphasis from acontextual writing classes to the socialization of students into the communications of their disciplines . . . through communications intensive (CI) programs."[8]

Additionally, faculty responses on "perceived student deficiencies in writing; activities not practiced currently in courses to improve writing; and resources faculty find helpful are: a writing center, guidance on revising from a technical writer, and instruction on how to create an excellent paper."[9]

Describing assessment in chapter 6 from Collins's report is a detailed rubric evaluating Independent Writing in a gas turbines research project. Professor Sarnaki, the rubric's composer, also assigns weekly research on the origin of industrial acronyms.[10] These specifics in learning the titles of new technological advances update and enhance background knowledge. An important thinking component of writing terminology is incorporated in his instruction.

The college requires Technical Communications, a writing course, for all engineering students. Management Communications and Oral Communications Skills are mandatory for business students, while Composition is a requisite course for every student. As at Duke University, discipline-specific writing emphasizes thinking skills. Additionally, more demanding curriculum extensions, such as the honors program, have been established.

The importance of writing in engineering is verified by practical necessity, including design explanations and limitations, as well as extensive safety reports. Considerations of

CHAPTER 9

international standards, as well as STCW requirements for licensing and certifications, in addition to program accreditation for the college, entails written communication, explains Professor Laurie Flood, department chair.[11]

Furthermore, in reporting his assessment techniques, professor of Technical Communications Paul Wlodkowski maintains: "In general, students need better preparation in grammar, style and organizing their thoughts in a clear and analytical way. The technical proposal is the most writing intensive assignment.... This is one of the most challenging courses to teach.... I enjoy it, and believe strongly in the power of writing for advancement in the profession."[12]

Yacht designer Chuck Paine agrees. In his 2010 book *My Yacht Designs: And What They Taught Me*, Paine claims: "I majored in Engineering, and as I like to tell people, I minored in sailing.... I honed my writing skills. I don't think there's ever been a successful yacht designer who wasn't also a facile writer—writing is imperative in the yacht design game."[13]

Establishing the design requirements as requested and necessary for the yacht buyer necessitates numerous contacts. Usually, inquiries and proposals are written communication, so all involved may refer to actual statements. Writing shows the thoughts and intentions of both. The communications focus on understanding and agreement, as the vision of the designer merges with the customer's dream of a beautiful yacht.

Paine explains:

> The driving force behind the *Whistler 48* was the pilothouse. In a way, this pilothouse was a watershed for me. I could make it more practical with taller forward windows, or make it prettier by keeping the pilothouse low. For the rest of my career, I worshipped at the altar of beauty and threw practicality to the winds when the two conflicted.[14]

WRITING ON OTHER EDUCATIONAL LEVELS

Only when a meticulously conceived idea is agreed upon, will a marine designer move forward in his conception. Significantly, a written contract is then prepared and signed for verification on agreement. Additions and adjustments are stipulated in writing as necessary.

For more than a decade, in addition to designing yachts, Paine wrote articles for *Cruising World*, and other yachting publications to supplement his income. He received more than a paycheck—free publicity—by illustrating his articles with drawings of his designs.[15]

Not only when creating a proposal for a yacht concept to fulfill design criteria for the ideal America's Cup contender, a dependable blue water cruising vessel, or a graceful sailing sloop is a written description of every detail required. Judicious estimations of supplies, labor, and time are based on the precise calculations written by the designer. The cost is determined through the written description, including the process and classifications itemized. Contractors bid based on the designer's written information.

Builders and craftsmen, from mechanics and welders to painters and carpenters, will refer diligently to the initial drawing, and subsequent ones. Paine says:

> As soon as the drawings were done, and I was once again unemployed, I went to work for *Harry's* builder as a boat carpenter. It's not a bad thing to design a boat and then see whether the drawings tell the builder everything he needs to know, because [now] you *are* the builder. Work as a boat builder, and you'll learn what you need to show him.[16]

Dimensions, materials, and mechanical systems from sails and hydraulics to ventilation and plumbing, appliances, and furnishings require written specifications to explain the requirements and process for what is built above, on, and

CHAPTER 9

below deck. The layers of drawings for every component require not only written numbers, but also accurate descriptions to ensure precise installation.

A yacht is an especially complex engineering problem: like a building, a vessel uses a variety of materials, weathers climate changes, and must meet all necessary construction codes. Unlike a building, not only must a yacht move, but it must withstand various water pressures, temperatures, and liquid impermeability, all within a confined space.

For example, in hydraulics, all flow and psi/kPa (pounds per square inch/kilos Pascal) of applicable fluid must be listed. Included are the dimensions of piping or hoses carrying the fluid, the capacity of the complete system, as well as reservoirs created or reduced when the various parts, such as the steering, are activated. From winches to stateroom plumbing, hydraulic power is used throughout to make the mechanics run smoothly and function with ease.

Written language and numerics are necessary for creating, not only an idea, but also construction. Hydraulic history, theory, and terminology are contained in the directions for building and completing. Safety and certification for all the systems must also be analyzed and verified, not only when building and testing, but also during the final evaluation before delivery, when the vessel actually sails for the first time—known as "sea trials"—occur.

As with interesting writing, aesthetics enhance viewer response. Aesthetics are complementary to the yacht's integrity, as are its stability and safety. In yacht design, aesthetics are most important; desirable yacht imperatives begin with beauty. Paine states

> Erica was conceived to add beauty to the world. . . . I drew yachts because when I managed to get the curves just right, I was staring at something intrinsically beautiful. In the final

WRITING ON OTHER EDUCATIONAL LEVELS

analysis, it's their beauty that justifies yachts' existence and considerable expense.[17]

Thinking through writing with drawing creates insight and new knowledge in the design of a yacht. In-depth thinking produces the concept, extends the details, and completes the ideas.

Professional writing is a necessary tool, as important as any mechanical device, in conception and construction. Showing thinking through writing is required on all professional levels. As Zull attests: "Language is the primary way we change ideas into actions."[18]

AFTERWORD

Writing is thinking, writing is learning...
—National Writing Project teacher participant

In 2014, the president of the University of Vermont wrote "The first of six learning outcomes developed by the faculty within the general education criteria is communication, writing and information literacy."[1] Collins's report on communications in engineering lists clear writing as a required outcome for engineering majors. Chuck Paine, a yacht designer, attests to the professional necessity of writing.

As a universal goal in education, writing is essential. "To convince us that writing belongs at the center of a university curriculum ... is to let us experience its power. (And satisfaction),"[2] wrote a teacher participating in the National Writing Project. On all educational levels, instructors in every discipline acknowledge the use of writing to improve thinking skills and enhance comprehension of content and its application.

Thinking and writing converge on the longitude and latitude of learning. As each learner embarks on the sea of words, education sets sail on writing to reach its destination. The Composition course syllabus offers William Zinsser's advice for the voyage: "Words are the only tools you will be given. Learn to use them with originality and care."[3]

NOTES

CHAPTER 1

1. Janet Emig, "Writing as a Mode of Learning," *College Composition and Communication* 28, No. 2 (1977), 124-25, 127.
2. Ibid.
3. Tom Sullivan, "On the Value of a Liberal Education," *Vermont Quarterly*, No. 70 (2015), 63.
4. James E. Zull, *The Art of Changing the Brain* (Sterling, VA: Stylus Publishing, 2002), 201.
5. Ibid., 207.
6. Ibid., 242.
7. Ibid.
8. Toby Fulwiler, *Teaching With Writing* (Portsmouth, NH: Heinnemann, 1987), 44.
9. Ann Bertoff, quoted in Fulwiler, *Teaching With Writing* (Portsmouth, NH: Heinnemann, 1987), 5.
10. Emig, "Writing as a Mode of Learning," *College Composition And Communication* 28, No. 2 (May, 1977): 122.

NOTES

CHAPTER 2

1. John Barlow, ed., *Maine Maritime Academy College Catalogue* (Castine, ME: 2007-2009), 3.
2. John J. Collins, *The Effective Writing Teacher* (Columbus, OH: ERIC, 1989), 17.
3. Carol W. Benton, *Thinking About Thinking* (Lantham, MD: Rowman and Littlefield Education, 2014), 8.
4. Ibid., 139.
5. Ibid., 140.
6. William Zinsser, *On Writing Well* (New York: Harper and Row Publishers, 1976), 7.
7. Arthur A. Costa and Lawrence F. Lowery, *Techniques for the Teaching of Thinking* (Pacific Grove, CA: Critical Thinking Press, 1989), 16, 17.
8. Thomas S. Kane, *The New Oxford Book of Writing* (Oxford: Oxford University Press, 1988), 210.
9. Laurie C. Stone, *Oral Report Rubric* (Castine, ME: Maine Maritime Academy, 2008), 1.
10. Sam Lagrone, ed., "You Have To Be A Good Thinker," *Proceedings* 141, No. 1, 350 (2015), 16-21.
11. Harrison Scramm, "Constructive, Not Disruptive, Thinking," *Proceedings* 141, No. 1, 350 (2015), 10.
12. Sam LaGrone, ed., "General Prize Essay Contest," *Proceedings* 141, No. 1, 350 (2015), 27.

CHAPTER 4

1. Emig, "Writing as a Mode of Learning," 126.
2. John C. Bean, *Engaging Ideas*, Second Edition (San Francisco: Jossey Bass, 2011), 27-28.
3. John Dewey, *How We Think* (New York: D. C. Heath and Company, 1933), 40.
4. Zull, *The Art of Changing the Brain*, 202.

NOTES

5. John Dewey, *Education and Experience* (New York: Simon and Schuster, 1938), 75.

CHAPTER 5

1. Emig, "Writing as a Mode of Learning," 125.

CHAPTER 6

1. Fulwiler, *Teaching With Writing,* 86-87.
2. Bean, *Engaging Ideas,* 211-12.
3. Ibid., 34.
4. Ken Bain, *What The Best College Teachers Do* (Cambridge, MA: Harvard University Press, 2004), 22.
5. Fulwiler, *Teaching With Writing,* 97.
6. Bean, *Engaging Ideas,* 35.
7. Peter Sarnacki, "Term Paper Guidelines," in Stephen A. Collins, "Communications in Engineering." (Castine, ME: Maine Maritime Academy 2009), 24.
8. Zinsser, *On Writing Well,* 31.

CHAPTER 7

1. Stephen Tchudi, *Teaching Writing in Content Areas: College Level* (West Haven, CT: NEA Professional Library, 1986), 60.
2. Sarnaki, "Term Paper Guidelines," 23.
3. Ibid., p. 24.
4. Stephen A. Collins, "Communications in Engineering" (Castine, ME: Maine Maritime Academy, 2009), 19.
5. Stephen Debruyn, "Using Recognition To Increase Student Achievement" (Manhattan, KS: The Master Teacher, 2007), No. 15, 1.

NOTES

6. Marcia Birkin, "Using Writing to Assist Learning in Mathematics Classes," in *Writing to Learn Mathematics and Science*, eds., Paul Connolly and Teresa Villardi (New York: Teachers College Press, 1989), 39.

7. Fulwiler, *Teaching With Writing*, 104.

8. Nobel, Alfred, *His Last Will and Testament*, 1895.

CHAPTER 8

1. Fulwiler, *Teaching With Writing*, 44.
2. James Van Allen quoted in Bean, *Engaging Ideas*, 97, 98.
3. Emig, "Writing as a Mode of Learning," 125.
4. Fulwiler, *Teaching With Writing*, 1, 3-5.
5. Marwine, Alan, "Reflection on the Uses of Informal Writing," in *Writing to Learn Mathematics and Science*, Paul H. Connolly and Teresa Vilardi, eds. (New York: Teachers College Press, 1988), 61.
6. Ibid., 63.
7. Emig, "Writing as a Mode of Learning," 122.
8. Benton, *Thinking About Thinking*, 12-13.
9. Ibid., 10.
10. Colwell, quoted in Benton, *Thinking about Thinking*, 4.
11. Benton, *Thinking About Thinking*, 5.
12. Ibid., 36.
13. Benton, *Thinking About Thinking*, 12-13.
14. Ibid., 10.
15. Colwell, quoted in Benton, *Thinking About Thinking*, 4.
16. Benton, *Thinking About Thinking*, 5.
17. Shaham, Orli, interview by Diane Rehm, "The Diane Rehm Show," WAMU 88.5, Washington, DC. July 22, 2014.
18. Benton, *Thinking About Thinking*, 40.
19. Beth Staples, "Click," *UMaine Today*, No. 1 (January, 2015), 43.
20. Mark S. Andrews, "The Nature of Light Curriculum" (Farmington, ME: University of Maine at Farmington), 1.
21. Marwine, "Reflections on the Use of Informal Writing," 61.
22. Andrews, "Curriculum Design," 12.

NOTES

23. William J. Mullin, "Qualitative Thinking and Writing in the Hard Sciences," *Writing to Learn Science and Mathematics*, Paul H. Connolly and Teresa Vilardi, eds., (New York: Teachers College Press, 1988), 201.
24. Ibid.
25. Ibid.
26. Kemp, Peter, ed., *The Oxford Companion to Ships and the Sea*, (New York: Oxford University Press, 1988), 204.
27. Holyoak, Keith J. and Robert G. Morison, eds., *The Complete Oxford Handbook To Thinking and Reasoning* (Oxford: Oxford University Press, 2012), 7.
28. Marwine, "Reflections on the Use of Informal Writing," 62.
29. Ibid., 63.
30. Gopen, George D. and David A. Smith, "What's an Assignment Like You Doing in a Course Like This? Writing in Mathematics," *Writing to Learn Mathematics and Science*, Paul H. Connolly and Teresa Vilardi, eds. (New York: Teachers College Press, 1988), 210.
31. Ibid., 22.
32. Bean, *Engaging Ideas*, 27.
33. Marcia Birkin, "Using Writing to Assist Learning in Mathematics Classes," *Writing to Learn Mathematics and Science*, Paul H. Connolly and Teresa Vilardi, eds. (New York: Teachers College Press, 1989), 36, 42.
34. Ibid.
35. Ibid., 39.
36. Ibid., 41-42.
37. Ibid.

CHAPTER 9

1 Sally Leighton, telephone interviews by the author, 11-12. 2015.
2. Ibid.
3. C. B. Olsen, quoted in *Techniques for the Teaching of Thinking* (Pacific Grove, CA: Critical Thinking Press, 1989), 23.

NOTES

4. Emig, "Writing as a Mode of Learning," 122.
5. Bean, *Engaging Ideas*, 27.
6. Dean Drenk, quoted in Bean's *Engaging Ideas*, p.75.
7. Emig, "Writing as a Mode of Learning," 125.
8. Stephen A. Collins, "Communications in Engineering," 1.
9. Ibid., 2.
10. Sarnaki, "Term Paper Guidelines," 34.
11. Laurie Flood, telephone interview by author, December 10, 2015.
12. Paul A. Wlodkowski, "Assessment," in Collins, "Communications in Engineering," 35-36.
13. Chuck Paine, *My Yacht Designs* (Camden, ME: Chuck Paine.com Publications, 2010), 3.
14. Ibid., 48.
15. Ibid., 19.
16. Ibid., 225.
17. Ibid., 260.
18. Zull, *The Art of Changing the Brain*, 208.

AFTERWORD

1. Sullivan, "The Value of a Liberal Education," 63.
2. Fulwiler, *Teaching With Writing*, 154.
3. Zinsser, *On Writing Well*, 35.

BIBLIOGRAPHY

Applebee, Arthur N. and Judith A. Langer. *How Writing Shapes Thinking.* Urbana, Illinois: NCTE, 1987.

Andrews, Mark S. "Curriculum Design." Farmington, Maine: University of Maine at Farmington, 1973.

Andrews, Mark S. "The Nature of Light Curriculum." Farmington, Maine: The University of Maine at Farmington, 1973.

Angelo, Thomas A. and K. Patricia Cross. *Classroom Assessment Techniques: A Handbook for College Teachers.* Second Edition. San Francisco: Jossey Bass, 1993.

Aristotle, *The Rhetoric.*

Bacon, Francis. "Of Studies," *The Essays.* New York, NY: Penguin Classics, 1986.

Bain, Ken. *What The Best College Teachers Do.* Cambridge, Massachusetts: Harvard University Press, 2004.

Barlow, John, ed. *Maine Maritime Academy College Catalogue, 2007-2009.* Castine, Maine: Maine Maritime Academy, 2007.

Bean, John C. *Engaging Ideas.* Second Edition. San Francisco: Jossey Bass, 2011.

Bechtel, Judith. *Improving Writing and Learning.* Boston: Allyn and Bacon, 1985.

Benton, Carol. *Thinking About Thinking.* Lantham, Maryland: Rowman and Littlefield Education, 2014.

BIBLIOGRAPHY

Bertoff, Ann. *Teaching With Writing.* Toby Fulwiler. Portsmouth, New Hampshire: Heinnemann, 1987.

Beston, Henry. *The Outermost House.* New York: Macmillan, 1928.

Beyer, Barry K. *Practical Strategies for the Teaching of Thinking.* Boston: Allyn and Bacon, 1987.

Birkin, Marcia. "Using Writing to Assist Learning in Mathematics Classes." In *Writing to Learn Mathematics and Science.* Paul H. Connolly and Teresa Vilardi, eds. New York: Teachers College Press, 1989.

Britton, James, et al. *The Development of Writing Abilities.* London: Macmillan, 1975.

Byrne, Donn. *Teaching Writing Skills.* New York: Longman, 1979.

Carson, Rachel. *The Sea Around Us.* Cambridge: Oxford University Press, 1951.

Collins, John J. *The Effective Writing Teacher.* Columbus, Ohio: ERIC, 1989.

Collins, Stephen A. "Communications in Engineering." Castine, Maine: Maine Maritime Academy, 2008.

Conrad, Joseph. *The Heart of Darkness, Youth, End of the Tether.* Cambridge: Cambridge University Press, 2010.

Conrad, Joseph. *The Mirror of the Sea.* Collected Works Of Joseph Conrad. Volume II. Dent, 1949.

Connolly, Paul and Teresa Villardi, eds. *Writing To Learn Mathematics and Science.* New York: Teachers College Press, 1989.

Cooper, S. et al. *Writing Logically, Thinking Critically.* New York: Routledge, 1978.

Corbett, Edward P. J., Nancy Myers, Gary Tate. *The Writing Teacher's Sourcebook.* New York: Oxford University Press, 1994.

Costa, Arthur A. and Lawrence F. Lowery. *Techniques for the Teaching of Thinking.* Pacific Grove, California: Critical Thinking Press, 1989.

Debruyn, Robert L. *Using Recognition to Increase Student Achievement.* Manhattan, Kansas: The Master Teacher, 2007.

Dewey, John. *How We Think.* New York, DC: Heath and Company, 1933.

Dewey, John. *Education and Experience.* New York: Simon and Schuster, 1938.

Drenk, Dean. "Teaching Finance Through Writing." In *Teaching Writing in All Disciplines*, C. W. Giffin, ed. New Directions for Teaching and Learning, No. 12. San Francisco: Jossey Bass, 1986.

BIBLIOGRAPHY

Emig, Janet. "Writing as a Mode of Learning." *College Composition and Communication.* Volume 28, No. 2 (May, 1977): 122-28.

Flood, Laurie. Telephone interview by the author, December 10, 2015.

Flower, Linda. *Problem Solving Strategies for Writing.* New York: Harcourt, Brace, Jovanovich, Inc., 1981.

Fulwiler, Toby. *Teaching With Writing.* Portsmouth, NH: Heinnemann, 1987.

Goodridge, Henry and Lew Dietz. *Andre the Seal.* Camden, Maine: Downeast Books, 1975.

Harris, Muriel. *Prentice Hall Reference Guide.* Upper Saddle River, New Jersey: Pearson Prentice Hall, 2007.

Helker, Paul. *The Essay: Theory and Pedagogy for an Active Form.* Urbana, Illinois: NCTE, 1996.

Holyoak, Keith J. and Robert G. Morison, eds. *The Oxford Handbook of Thinking and Reasoning.* New York: Oxford University Press, 2012.

Kane, Thomas S., ed. *The New Oxford Book of Writing.* Oxford: Oxford University Press. 1988.

Kemp, Peter, ed. *The Oxford Companion to Ships and the Sea.* New York: Oxford University Press, 1988.

Kenyon, R. W. "Writing Is Problem Solving." In *Writing to Learn Mathematics and Science.* Paul H. Connolly and Teresa Vilardi, eds. New York: Teachers College Press, 1988.

Lagrone, Sam. "You Have To Be A Good Thinker." *Proceedings.* 141 (August, 2015), pp. 16-21.

Leighton, Sally. Telephone interviews by the author. November-December, 2015; August, 2016.

Loomis, Susan K. *Composition Syllabus.* Castine, Maine: Maine Maritime Academy, 2008.

Marwine, Alan. "Reflections on the Uses of Informal Writing." In *Writing to Learn Mathematics and Science.* Paul H. Connolly and Teresa Vilardi, eds. New York: Teachers College Press, 1988.

McKenna, Robert. *The Dictionary of Nautical Literacy.* Camden, Maine: International Marine, 2001.

McPhee, John. *Irons in the Fire.* New York: Farrar, Strauss and Giroux, 1997.

McPhee, John. *Looking for a Ship.* New York: Farrar, Stroux, Giroux. 1990.

McWhorter, Kathleen T. *Study and Critical Thinking in College.* New York: Pearson/Longman, 2008.

BIBLIOGRAPHY

Mowat, Farley. *The Grey Seas Under.* Guilford, Connecticut: The Lyons Press, 1958.

Paine, Charles. *My Yacht Designs.* Camden, Maine: Chuck Paine.com Publications, 2010.

Raban, Jonathan, ed. *The Oxford Book of the Sea.* Oxford: Oxford University Press, 1993.

Roberts, Kenneth. *Don't Say That About Maine.* Portland: Anthoensen Press, 1986.

Safina, Carl. *Song for a Blue Ocean.* New York: Holt, 1998.

Scramm, Harrison. "Constructive, Not Disruptive Thinking." *Proceedings.* 141 (August, 2015), 10.

Shaham, Orli, interview by Diane Rehm. "The Diane Rehm Show." WAMU 88.5, Washington, DC. July 22, 2014.

Staples, Beth. "Click." *UMaine Today,* 15 (January, 2015), 40-43.

Stone, Laurie C. *Oral Report Rubric.* Castine, Maine: Maine Maritime Academy, 2008.

Strong, Prentice III and Twain Braden. *In Peril.* Guilford, Connecticut: Lyons Press, 2004.

Sullivan, Tom. "On the Value of a Liberal Education." *Vermont Quarterly,* 70 (March, 2014), 2, 63.

Tchudi, Stephen. *Teaching Writing in Content Areas: College Level.* West Haven, Connecticut: NEA Professional Library, 1986.

Zinsser, William. *On Writing Well.* New York: Harper Collins, 2001.

Zinsser, William. *Writing To Learn.* New York: Harper Collins, 1988.

Zull, James A. *The Art of Changing the Brain.* Sterling, Virginia: Stylus Publishing, 2002.

INDEX

active exploratory writing, 69
American Mathematical Society (AMS), 113
The American Practical Navigator (Bowditch), 72.
   See also *Bowditch's Navigation* (Bowditch)
American Psychological Association (APA), style, 113
American Red Cross, 28, 74
AMS. *See* American Mathematical Society
Andre the Seal (Goodridge), 40, 46, 80
Andrews, Mark S., 140-42, 144
The Arcturus Adventure, 26-27, 36
argument, 45-47, 80, 102;
   reasoning in, 46-47;
   warrant of, 46
argumentative writing, 45

Bain, Ken, 109
Barlow, John, 10
Bascom, Willard, 18, 29, 92, 96
Bean, John C., 65, 108, 114-15, 155
Beaufort, Sir Francis, 27, 73
The Beaufort Scale, 27, 73
Beebe, William, 26-27, 36, 94-95, 98
Benton, Carol W., 15-16, 137-39, 138-39
Bertoff, Ann, 6
Beston, Henry, 11, 18, 42, 92
Birkin, Marcia, 127
Birkin, Marian, 148
Bowditch, Nathaniel, 20, 72, 93
Bowditch's Navigation (Bowditch), 72.
   See also *The American Practical Navigator* (Bowditch)
Bowdoin (Thorndike), 12
brain:
   emotions and, 4;

motivation and, 4;
motor, 4;
seeing, 3;
visual, 3-4
brain functions, thinking skills elements coordination with, 5-7

Carson, Rachel, 11, 18, 20, 37, 92-93, 99
cause and effect, 36-37
Chase, Andy, 11, 38, 72
Chicago Manual of Style (CMS), 113
Cicero, 1
"The Circulation of the Oceans," 27
clarity, in thesis-guided formal writing, 113
classification, 27-28
CMS. *See* Chicago Manual of Style
Collins, John J., 13
Collins, Stephen A., 159, 165
Columbus, Christopher, 51, 97
Colwell, Richard, 138
comments:
neutral, 127-28;
positive, 126
"Communications in Engineering," 159
compare and contrast, 35-36
complexity quote, 20
Conrad, Joseph, 11-12, 29, 36, 48, 98, 114, 130
content:
thinking about, 3;
through writing in a genre, 88-89
corrections and comments supporting grading, 126-28;
neutral comments, 127-28;
positive comments, 126
Costa, Arthur, 9, 19, 105
Council of Science Editors (CSE), 113
Cruising World, 161
CSE. *See* Council of Science Editors
curriculum:
classification and, 27;
creating similar assessment criteria across, 122-23;
essay exam questions in, 128-29;
expressive writing and, 65-66;
maritime, 10, 52

Dana, Richard Henry, 26, 94
Darwin, Charles, 18, 45, 80, 92
DeBruyn, Robert L., 126
description, as writing genres, 16-21;
complexity quote, 20;
exploratory writing, 19-20;
formal writing, 20-21;
independent writing, 21;
maritime literary selections as models, 18-19;
reinforcing experience, 17
Dewey, John, 66-67, 151
The Dictionary of Nautical Literacy (McKenna), 12

division, 26-27
documentation, in thesis-guided formal writing, 112-13
"Don't Say That About Maine," 47, 91
Drenk, Dean, 155
Duke University, 159
The Dynamics of the Ocean's Surface, 18, 29

education:
  higher, 3;
  music, 137-39;
  precollege, 152-55;
  writing as a universal goal in, 165
Emerson, Ralph Waldo, 40, 101
Emig, Janet, 1-2, 7, 53, 65, 85-86, 133, 137, 145, 151, 153, 157
The English Admirals, 40
English Traits, 40
essay exam question examples, 130-31
essay exams, composing, 129-32;
  essay exam question examples, 130-31;
  evaluate exam questions, 131;
  ideal evaluation for thinking skills instruction, 131-32
example of planning exploratory writing, 82-83
exam questions, evaluating, 131
Exploratory Writing, 19-20, 23;
  active, 69;
  activities, 66-67;
  example of planning, 82-83;
  forms, 68;
  independent writing and, 108-10;
  in other disciplines, 134-35;
  thinking exercises, 70-80
exploratory writing thinking exercises template, 81
Expressive Writing, 65, 134. *See also* Exploratory Writing

Father and Son, 37
Flood, Laurie, 160
Formal Writing, 20-21, 24;
  additional exercises using essays, 90-91;
  creating a thesis, 86-87;
  maritime literature examples and topics, 92-103;
  thesis-guided, 110-13;
  thinking about content through writing in a genre, 88-89;
  thinking exercises for, 90;
  thinking skills in, 88
Formal Writing perspectives, 135-37
Fowles, John, 35, 76
Fulwiler, Toby, 6, 106, 110, 128, 133-34

genre instruction, 26-31
Global Positioning System (GPS), 26-27, 39, 72
Goodridge, Henry, 40, 46, 80, 101
Gopen, George D., 147
Gosse, Edmund, 37, 99
GPS. *See* Global Positioning System

INDEX

The Grey Seas Under (Mowat), 11-12, 20, 47, 71
group oral report, 37-39

Harris, Muriel, 11
HMS Frisky, 20, 71

Independent Writing, 21, 25, 105-15;
concluding statements, 114-15;
exploratory writing, 108-10;
Learner Generated Inquiry, 108-10;
thesis-guided formal writing, 110-13;
thinking preparation for writing, 106-8
individual oral reports, 30-31
Informal Writing, 134, 146.
See also Exploratory Writing
In Peril (Strong), 11-12, 29, 36
inquiry, encouraging, 14-16
instructing the writing genres, 16-21
Irons in the Fire (McPhee), 33

Junger, Sebastian, 38

Kane, Thomas S., 28
Kemp, Peter, 12

Learner Generated Inquiry, 108-10
Leighton, Sally, 152-53
Looking for a Ship (McPhee), 11-12, 17, 20, 29-30, 70, 72

Loomis, Susan K., 11
lower-order incompetence, 118

marine environment, 43
marine resources, 42
marine transportation, 44-45
maritime literary selections as models, 18-19
maritime literature, using, 51-52
maritime literature examples and topics:
Formal Writing, 92-103
Marwine, Alan, 54, 134-35, 144, 146, 149
Massachusetts Maritime Academy, 38
mathematics:
thinking in, 145-50;
writing in, 145-50
McKenna, R. A., 12
McPhee, John, 11, 17, 20, 29-30, 33, 44, 66, 70-75, 89, 91, 93
metacognition, 2, 13, 34, 45, 50, 55, 115, 137-38
midterm activities, 32-34;
midterm exam, 33;
midterm writing evaluation, 34;
research paper preparation and individual conferences, 33;
research seminar, 32
The Mirror of the Sea (Conrad), 12, 48, 114
Modern Language Association (MLA) style, 113

INDEX

Morison, Samuel Eliot, 12, 20, 37, 40, 77, 93, 101
Mowat, Farley, 11, 20, 47, 71, 102
Mullins, William J., 145
Munk, Walter, 27, 73
music education:
 thinking in, 137-39;
 writing in, 137-39
My Yacht Designs: And What They Taught Me (Paine), 160

The Narcissus, 36
nature of light, 141-42;
 thinking skills exercises from, 143-45
neutral comments, 127-28
Nobel, Alfred, 132

Old Bruin, 40
Olson, C. B., 153
oral reports, 24;
 group, 37-39;
 individual, 30-31
The Outermost House (Beston), 11-12, 18
The Oxford Book of the Sea, 11
The Oxford Book of Writing, 28
The Oxford Companion to Ships and the Sea, 12

Paine, Chuck, 112, 160-62, 165
The Perfect Storm, (Junger), 38
persuasion, 39-41
Phillips, Richard, 38
plagiarism, 108, 115
positive comments, 126

post-college thinking, and writing, 157
Powell, Colin, 51
precollege education, 152-55
The Prentice Hall Reference Guide (Harris), 11
preparatory writing, 13-14, 22;
 thinking in, 13-14
preparatory writing forms, 61
primary research sources, 111-12
primary traits analysis, 121
proactive assessment:
 composing essay exams, 129-32;
 creating similar assessment criteria across the curriculum, 122-23;
 criteria, 119-21;
 effective corrections and comments supporting grading, 126-28;
 grading points, 121-22;
 higher-order concerns, 119;
 lower-order concerns, 118;
 primary traits analysis, 121;
 thinking in exams, 128-29;
 thinking through writing assessment, 124-25
Proceedings, 51
process analysis, 28-29
professional thinking, and writing, 159-63

Raban, Jonathan, 11
reading and resources, 11-13
research paper, 25, 48-49

INDEX

research sources:
  primary, 111-12;
  secondary, 112
Roberts, Kenneth, 47, 91, 102

Safina, Carl, 11, 20, 40, 43, 47, 79, 93, 102
Sailing Alone around the World, 27, 29
Sarnacki, Peter, 114
SATs. *See* Scholastic Aptitude Tests
Scholastic Aptitude Tests (SATs), 152
sciences:
  thinking in, 140;
  writing in, 140
Scramm, Harrison, 52
"The Sea and the Wind That Blows," 30, 75, 89
The Sea around Us (Carson), 11-12, 18, 20, 37
secondary research sources, 112
sensory cortex, 4
Shaham, Orli, 139
Shipwreck (Fowles), 35, 76
Slocum, Joshua, 27, 29, 95-96
Smith, David A., 147
Smith, Michelle, 140
Song for the Blue Ocean (Safina), 11-12, 20, 40
Spring Tides (Morison), 12, 20, 37
Standards of Training, Certification and Watchkeeping (STCW), 9, 157, 160

STCW. *See* Standards of Training, Certification and Watchkeeping
Stevenson, Robert Louis, 40, 101
Stone, Laurie C., 31
The Story of Mount Desert Island, 12
Strong, Skip, 11, 29, 36, 96, 98
Sullivan, Tom, 3

Tchudi, Stephen, 119
thesis:
  creating, 86-87;
  forming, 110-11
thesis-guided formal writing, 110-13;
  clarity, 113;
  correct documentation, 112-13;
  forming a thesis, 110-11;
  presenting evidence, 111;
  primary research sources, 111-12;
  secondary research sources, 112
thinking:
  defined, 4
  exercises for Formal Writing, 90
  in mathematics, 145-50;
  in music education, 137-39;
  in preparatory writing, 13-14, 106-8;
  in the sciences, 140
thinking skills:
  in Formal Writing, 88;
  writing courses and, 7-8

thinking skills elements:
  with Exploratory Writing, 158;
  with Formal Writing, 158;
  with Independent Writing, 158;
  for instruction, 156-57;
  with learning activities, 22-23;
  with Preparatory Writing, 158
thinking skills instruction, 131-32
Thorndike, Virginia, 12
"Travels of the Rock," 89
Tugboats (Thorndike), 12
Two Years Before the Mast, 26

ultimate thinking, 105-15

Van Allen, James, 133
visual brain, 3-4
vocabulary, as component of writing, 3
The Voyage of the Beagle, 18

What the Best College Teachers Do (Bain), 109
White, E. B., 30, 37, 75, 89-90, 97
Winnefield, James A., 51-52
Wlodkowski, Paul, 160
writing:
  exploratory, 19-20, 23;
  formal, 20-21, 24;
  independent, 21, 25;
  in mathematics, 145-50;
  in music education, 137-39;
  in other disciplines, 133-50;
  post-college thinking and, 157;
  precollege education, 152-55;
  preparatory, 13-14, 22;
  professional thinking and, 159-63;
  in the sciences, 140;
  thinking preparation for, 106-8;
  vocabulary as component of, 3
Writing Across the Curriculum movement, 3
writing assessment, thinking through, 124-25
writing courses, 7-8
writing genres:
  description, 16-21;
  instructing, 16-21
Wylie, C. C., 26, 72

Youth (Conrad), 11-12

Zinsser, William, 18, 115, 133
Zull, James E., 3-4, 65-66, 117, 132, 151, 163

ABOUT THE AUTHOR

K. A. Beals is an educational writer and college writing instructor, most recently at Maine Maritime Academy. She holds a BFA from Windham College, an MEd from the University Of Vermont, and is completing a PhD in Maritime Literature.

Beals has taught and tutored writing and literature since 1980 at Maine and Vermont colleges. She received the Janeway Arts Fellowship for poetry and painting, and revised an undergraduate laboratory manual through a National Science Foundation Grant. Beals is also the author of *Achieving College Success* and the forthcoming *Ocean Literacy Concepts*.

www.ingramcontent.com/pod-product-compliance
Lightning Source LLC
Chambersburg PA
CBHW021758230426
43669CB00006B/116